17.50

Southwestern Cooking
New & Old

Southwestern Cooking
New & Old

Ronald Johnson

University of New Mexico Press

Albuquerque

Design by Milenda Nan·Ok Lee

Library of Congress Cataloging in Publication Data

Johnson, Ronald, 1935–
  Southwestern cooking.

  Rev. ed. of: The aficionado's Southwestern cooking.
1st ed. 1968.
  Includes index.
  1. Cookery, American—Southwestern style. 2. Cookery,
Mexican. I. Johnson, Ronald, 1935– . Aficionado's
Southwestern cooking. II. Title.
TX715.J7 1985   641.59791   84-19603
ISBN 0-8263-0788-4

*This book is dedicated to
Gus Blaisdell, who first suggested it,
and those many friends who have
invited me to the Southwest
these many years.*

Contents

Introduction   1

Appetizers   5

Soups   29

Sauces and Garnishes   49

Tortilla Specialties   65

Eggs   99

Fish   113

Chicken and Turkey   123

Meats   141

Tamale Pies   165

Barbecues   175

Vegetables and Starches   187

Salads   215

Desserts   237

Ingredients   269

Menus   277

Index   285

Introduction

Our country's oldest cuisine is also its most exotic, echoing Mexico rather than neighbor states. Electric with chiles, full of sass and spice from native plants, made sound with corn and beans, these near timeless foods are barely noticed outside those states that keep it a sturdy part of the diet: New Mexico, Arizona, Texas, and parts of Colorado, Utah, Nevada, and California. Treasured since first settlers, it is cooked and savored daily from great ranch to humble adobe—both alike having at all times a bean pot on the back of the stove. No kitchen is without tortillas, or a string of dried chiles against the wall.

Lyndon Johnson campaigned his way to the White House by throwing great chili feeds. During his presidency chili was served at least once a week. When in Rome filming Cleopatra, *Elizabeth Taylor flew in bowls of chili from Chasen's, in Hollywood. (*Chile *being the name of pod and plant, but* chili *the name of both powder and "bowl of red.") Even a teenager here stops off for a taco after school rather than a hamburger and fries, and truckdrivers order huevos rancheros for early breakfast. What are the rest of us missing?*

Apparently three-quarters of the country, influenced by harsh bottled sauces and restaurants serving the same dull platter over and over, have (probably excusably) shrugged all this off as "Tex-Mex": a couple of fire-alarm sauces, some hamburger, cheese, a mess of beans and rice, shredded iceberg lettuce—maybe two olives or radishes tucked around the edge. The native knows better, smiling.

Even the lucky newcomer knows these people are serious about their tortillas, chile sauces. A first visitor ordering even breakfast eggs in New Mexico is faced with the question, "Red or Green?"—referring to the chile which will accompany the eggs. To be invited to dinner is to sample the house enchilada. Sooner or later this same newcomer will be advising outlanders that his/her cuisine boasts a complexity of flavors calculated to form addiction, cultivate admiration, prolong appetite, and greatly vary the simplest cupboard.

If this newcomer is also a cook, a whole new technique and file of recipes is called for. Soon after turning a first chimichanga, though, our now "chef" will

1

praise you that beloved trio of chile, bean, corn, on which Mozartian variations can be performed. You will be told how they seem to complete a nutritional whole as we know it today: incomplete protein grasping mirror incomplete protein. In effect this diet needs little if any meat to make you bounce and carry on. And yes, it is probably our best kept secret for healthy, inexpensive, tasty foods.

Once I was that newcomer. It has been fifteen years now a friend asked me to write a cookbook for the University of New Mexico Press, after he had eaten a weekend or two of meals. It was written, duly published handsomely, and continues to inform and please household cooks today. It is also the only book of mine which could be found, circa 1980, on a drugstore rack in downtown Roswell, New Mexico, alongside the likes of Irving Stone and Faulkner. I bought a copy—the clerk recommending it highly—and leafed through with new eyes. Not only did I now cook most recipes differently, I knew so many more. Some great classics had been overlooked, some new peaks been won.

While that book was written in the late sixties, Aspen, Colorado was still pretty much a backwater. I had to ride down to Glenwood Springs to get even a frozen tortilla. Living later in San Francisco's Mission district, I'd learned to use leaf coriander, fresh and dried chiles of a dozen kinds. There were black beans at hand to vary the trusty pinto, daily-made tortillas round the corner, carnitas and carne asada filling plump burritos down the block. On trips back to the Southwest I had discovered carne adovada, the world's best green chile sauce, a superior natillas. On and on. So it seemed best to sit down and write it right.

I've kept to the spirit of the old, however, in trying to keep this a simple manual for cooks without a fresh chile to choose from, shoppers without the hope of a ripe tomato, anyone before a stove with appetites to whet. Basic ingredients are likely to be found on the shelf of any large market—maybe not one in Boston proper, but many.

Once and always the newcomer, I have still ransacked the shelves of Fortnum's in London for tortillas and chile sauce. In France or Rome I would ever dream of a late lunch at Josie's around from Santa Fe's Plaza: first a bowl of steaming posole, then a taco platter made with blue tortillas, and a side of Josie's rich beans. Plenty of local color. I understand LBJ's and Miss Taylor's yen, and then some.

When home it is my special guest dinner, my preferred solitary lunch. Two tacquerías down the street know me by sight. I am drawn back and back to the Southwest to test its oldest and newest dishes, side by side. Everywhere I look others are curious about chiles and mesquite grills, seeking hints about how to dine there, where to go and what to order. Around the corner a block is shut down annually for an Indian festival with dancing and booths for Navajo fry bread with beans and red chile sauce. Santa Fe Grills open across the Bay, New York claims chiles are chic.

This is my answer, my kitchen.

San Francisco, 1984

Appetizers

They should be light, and surprise. They should lead on. They are both fattening and addictive. The French, with their planned five or six courses, consider them at most a stopgap—even their word hors d'oeuvres *suggests something "outside the work." Any Chinese meal seems to consist of a series of more or less equal appetizers. Everyone to his theory, I reckon. But I do know the typical Southwestern combination platter needs some prelude to warm us up. Even a fiesta of dishes merits a basket of homemade tortilla chips and a bowl of salsa to dip them in. And a buffet of the lot creates a buzz at any party.*

Tortilla Chips

These are also called tostados or tostaditos, but by whatever name they are delicious (particularly so to those who have never tasted anything but commercial tortilla chips). They are also ubiquitous: a basket of them is always served at home or in restaurants, to be dipped in fresh hot salsa, as an appetizer. They are used to scoop up and eat guacamole or refried beans. They are floated on soups, tossed with salads, layered in casseroles.

When cooking tortilla chips for a meal, plan on 3–4 corn tortillas per person—guests or family can go through an amazing amount. Stack tortillas and cut them in 8 pie-shaped wedges. Heat at least 1 inch of oil to a temperature of about 375°. If you don't have a thermometer, simply heat the oil until it starts to shimmer—it shouldn't smoke, for this breaks down the oil. Test one chip in the fat. The chip will be done when the fat stops bubbling. If the test chip is still chewy rather than crisp, the oil is not hot enough. If it turns brown, the fat is too hot.

Fry the chips in batches—just enough in a batch so the pan is not overcrowded. They can be served hot or at room temperature.

Nachos

Nachos begin with a base of tortilla chips, though the tortillas are usually cut in quarters rather than eighths. The simplest are ones spread out on a pan, after frying, and then sprinkled with grated Cheddar or Monterey Jack and a strip of green chile or sliced olives. These are then placed under a broiler until the cheese is melted. They should be served immediately.

For more complex versions, try these variations:

1. Sprinkle with cheese, then chili powder, before broiling.
2. Spread with refried beans, sprinkle with cheese, then top with strips of pickled jalapeños or mild green chile.
3. Spread with softened cream cheese, then top with fried crumbled chorizo and sliced ripe or green olives.
4. Spread with Picadillo (p. 153), then grated cheese. When the cheese melts top with cold Guacamole (p. 219) or sour cream.

Probably the variations are endless, but they should not be so complex they cannot be turned out and eaten while they are still hot and crisp.

Bean Dip I

4 cups cooked pinto beans (or
  black beans)
1 clove garlic, minced
2 tablespoons bacon fat (or butter)
1 tablespoon Worcestershire sauce
3–4 pickled jalapeños, seeded and
  minced

Remove beans from the pot with a slotted spoon; reserve liquid. Put beans through a food mill (or purée in a food processor). Sauté garlic in fat 3 minutes over low heat, and add it to the beans with all the other ingredients. Mash well (or give a few quick whirls in a processor) and add enough liquid from the bean pot to make the dip moist. Serve warm with tortilla chips.
Serves 6–8

After you've tasted this you'll forget about commercial bean dips. A variation is to stir in 1 cup grated Cheddar or Monterey Jack until it melts in the warm beans.

Bean Dip II

1 cup Refried Beans (p. 60)
1 cup sour cream
salt
Jalapeño Salsa (p. 56)

Prepare Refried Beans, and when they are just beginning to acquire a brown crust, add the sour cream. Stir it in until the mixture is hot all the way through. Add salt and jalapeño sauce to taste. Serve warm with tortilla chips.
Serves 4–6

A suave dip with a quite different character from Bean Dip I. I can't decide which I like best.

Cold Garbanzo Dip

1 pound dried garbanzos (or 2
   15-ounce cans)
3 tablespoons olive oil
1 cup onion, finely chopped
1 clove garlic, minced
¼ cup fresh coriander, minced (or
   parsley)
¼ cup piñon nuts
salt
sour cream

Soak garbanzos in plenty of water overnight, then simmer until tender. (Warning: they will require several hours of cooking.) Drain and put through a food mill (or purée in a food processor). Put oil in a small frying pan and sauté onions until soft over medium heat. As they cook, add the garlic, then the coriander or parsley. Finally, add the nuts and cook a few minutes more. Add to the garbanzos with salt to taste. Chill the mixture. At serving time add enough sour cream to make the dip moist. Serve with tortilla chips or strips of raw vegetables.

Serves 8–10

If you have the time to cook the garbanzos, fine, but canned garbanzos (also called chick-peas) have a good flavor and save time and energy. Whichever way you prepare this, though, you will have an unusual dip with an excellent nutty taste.

Gus's Mousse

3 avocados, seeded and peeled
1/4 cup Roquefort or blue cheese
1 1/2 tablespoons lemon juice
2 tablespoons cream
1/4 teaspoon Worcestershire sauce

"Mash all together, and put in a dish."

Serves 4–6

This Albuquerque dip may be the best, if most succinct. I surround it with radish "flowers" and tortilla chips.

Chile con Queso

2 tablespoons butter
1/4 cup green onions, minced with
  part of tops
1 cup tomatoes, chopped
1 4-ounce can green chiles,
  chopped
1/4 cup cream
1/2 pound Monterey Jack or
  Cheddar cheese, grated
salt
6 drops Tabasco sauce (or to taste)

Melt butter in a saucepan over medium heat. Sauté onion in butter until soft, then add tomatoes and chiles. Cook over low heat 15 minutes—or until all the liquid from the tomatoes is absorbed. Add cream, and when it begins to bubble, add the cheese. Stir constantly until the cheese is melted; don't let it boil. Add salt and Tabasco to taste. Serve in a chafing dish with tortilla chips.
Serves 6–8

The prototypical Southwestern dip, and one guests always dote on. Be careful to keep the flame in your chafing dish adjusted, though, for if the dish begins to bubble the cheese will get stringy.

Texas Caviar

2 cups dried black-eyed peas
salt
1 cup onion, chopped (green, red,
   or white)
2 cloves garlic, minced
1/4 cup vinegar
1/2 cup vegetable oil (or olive oil)
salt and freshly ground pepper
Tabasco sauce

Soak peas overnight (or use the quick soak method—see Beans, p. 269), then cook until tender in plenty of water. Dried black-eyed peas only take about 30 minutes to cook. When tender, add salt to taste and let sit 15 minutes or so to absorb the salt. Drain beans and mix while still warm with the rest of the ingredients. Tabasco sauce should be added to taste, but the dish ought not to be too hot. Chill covered in the refrigerator.
Serves 8–10

The Texans have taken the Southern black-eyed pea, hotted it up a little, and produced an appetizer which has become a favorite all over the country. In Texas they scoop it up with tortilla chips. Fresh or frozen black-eyed peas, often available, are more delicate and flavorful.

Jicama Sticks

1 medium jicama (about 4 inches
  wide)
4 limes
2 teaspoons salt
$1/2$ teaspoon chili powder (or to
  taste)

Peel off the thick outer rind of the jicama with a sharp knife, then peel the inner coating down to the white flesh. Cut into strips about the size of french fries and sprinkle with the juice of one of the limes. Serve with the rest of the limes cut into wedges and the salt and chili powder combined. Eat them by squeezing a little lime juice on, then dipping in the salt-and-chili-powder mixture.

Serves 6

Jicama is becoming increasingly popular all over the country and is more and more available. It looks like a large, bulbous sweet potato, and when peeled it has a bland, crisp flesh like a cross between an apple and a water chestnut.

Green Chile Won Tons

½ pound Monterey Jack cheese,
  grated
1 4-ounce can green chiles,
  chopped
1 package won ton wrappers
oil for frying
Guacamole (p. 219) (or Fresh Salsa
  [p. 55])

Combine cheese and chiles. Place about a teaspoon on a won ton wrapper. Moisten the edges of the wrappers—this is easiest done with a small brush—and fold like an envelope, pressing the edges together firmly. Fry in 2 inches hot oil until golden brown. Drain on paper towels. Serve with guacamole to dip them in.

Makes 30

If you can obtain the wrappers in your market, these make a great hot appetizer for a party. They can be put together well ahead of time, kept covered in the refrigerator, then fried in batches as you need them.

Green Chile Cheese Squares

1 4-ounce can green chiles,
  chopped
1 pound Cheddar cheese, grated
  (about 4 cups) (or 2 cups
  Cheddar and 2 cups Monterey
  Jack)
6 eggs, beaten
1/4 cup Parmesan cheese, grated
pitted ripe olive slices

Preheat oven to 350°. Butter sides and bottom of an 8-inch-square baking pan. Spread chiles on the bottom, sprinkle cheese over, then pour eggs over all. Sprinkle with the Parmesan, and bake 30 minutes—or until firm. Cut into 1-inch squares and top each square with a slice of olive. Serve warm with toothpicks for spearing.
Makes 64

A nice nibble for parties. For a buffet serve them on an attractive plate set on a warming tray.

Albondigas

¹/₂ pound ground beef
¹/₂ pound ground pork
²/₃ cup bread crumbs
1 egg, beaten
¹/₃ cup milk
¹/₃ cup cream
1 medium onion, minced
1 clove garlic, minced
4 pickled jalapeños, seeded and
    minced (or chili powder to taste)
¹/₂ teaspoon dried oregano
salt
oil for frying

Combine all the ingredients, with salt to taste. Roll into walnut-size balls. Fry in a little oil until browned on all sides. Serve hot in a chafing dish, with toothpicks for spearing.
Serves 8–10

Whenever meatballs are served at a party they seem to vanish like melting snow, for everyone seems to like them. These are particularly light with a little kick from the chiles, and to make them even hotter you can douse the mixture with a little Tabasco sauce before rolling the balls. They can be eaten as is or dipped in fresh salsa.

Chile Cashews

1¹/₂ tablespoons butter
2 cups cashew nuts
1 teaspoon salt
¹/₄ teaspoon powdered red chile
¹/₂ teaspoon ground cumin
¹/₂ teaspoon ground coriander

Melt butter in a frying pan over medium heat. Add the nuts and sauté for 3–4 minutes. Place nuts in a paper bag with salt, chile, and spices. Shake until the nuts are coated, then drain on paper towels.
Serves 4–6

This makes a spicy delight that disappears quick as a wink.

Oaxaca Bar Peanuts

2 tablespoons vegetable oil
8 cloves garlic, peeled and slightly
  flattened
8 small dried red chiles (optional)
1 pound raw shelled peanuts
1 teaspoon chili powder
1 teaspoon salt

Preheat oven to 300°. Put oil in a large frying pan (if you don't have one about 10″ make the nuts in two batches) and place over medium heat. Add garlic and chiles and cook, stirring and squashing down the garlic to release juices, until the garlic starts to turn gold. Add nuts, turn heat up high, and fry 3 minutes, turning and tossing constantly. Add chili powder and salt and cook another 1 minute, continuing to toss and turn. Don't overcook or the chili powder will burn. Pour out onto a cookie sheet. Bake 15 minutes. Let cool to room temperature, then store in an airtight container. The garlic and chiles can be removed if you like—

I leave them in because the garlic tastes maybe even better than the nuts. These are at their best after a day, and will keep for several weeks.

Serves 8–10

The legendary Oaxacan Bar Peanut is one dish we should immediately naturalize and call our own. They are irresistible and inexpensive, and since I discovered their secret I always keep a batch on hand. They make a nice gift, too, in a pretty cannister with a copy of the recipe. Raw peanuts can be found in the health-food section of a large market—I usually use the Spanish nut rather than the bigger ones since they seem to absorb more flavor.

Indian Nut Mix

oil for frying
1 corn tortilla, cut in ¹/₂-inch
   squares
1 flour tortilla, cut in ¹/₂-inch
   squares
salt
1 tablespoon butter
¹/₂ cup piñon nuts
¹/₂ cup pumpkin seeds
¹/₂ teaspoon red chile powder
¹/₄ teaspoon celery salt
¹/₄ teaspoon ground cumin

Preheat oven to 300°. Heat oil and fry the tortilla squares in batches. When they are crisp and golden, lift out with a slotted spoon onto paper towels. Salt immediately while they are hot. Melt butter in a small frying pan, and sauté piñon nuts and pumpkin seeds for several minutes—or until they start to pop and turn gold. Shake nuts and tortillas together in a paper bag with chile, celery salt, and cumin. Line a cookie sheet with paper towels, place the mixture on them, and bake for 10 minutes or until crisp.

Serves 4

A fine crisp nibble for all occasions. It is also a good way to use up leftover tortillas—in fact you might use just tortillas, omitting the nuts and seeds, and still have a tasty snack food.

Pickled Jalapeños Stuffed with Walnut Cheese

1 3-ounce package cream cheese
¹/₃ cup walnuts, finely chopped or
   ground
salt
6–8 pickled jalapeños

Cream the cheese with walnuts and salt to taste. Remove stems from the peppers and scoop out seeds. Stuff with the cheese mixture and refrigerate for several hours to firm the cheese. Slice into thin rings. It's difficult to say how many chiles you will need, as they come in different sizes. I usually pick out about six of the same size, and see how it goes.

Serves 4

These not only make an appetizer for those fond of the fiery jalapeño, but are also a pretty garnish to many a dish.

Ripe Olives Stuffed with Green Chile

1 6-ounce can pitted ripe olives
$1/4$ cup olive oil
1 tablespoon wine vinegar
1 teaspoon powdered red chile
$1/4$ teaspoon dried oregano
1 clove garlic, flattened
green chiles, cut into small strips

Drain olives and combine with all ingredients except green chiles. Let marinate, covered, in the refrigerator at least 24 hours. To serve, drain and stuff olives with green chile strip. Stick each olive with a toothpick to serve.

Serves 4

This recipe takes the tasteless ripe olive and turns it into something to write home about.

Escabeche of Shrimp

2/3 cup olive oil
1 cup red onions, chopped
3 cloves garlic, minced
2 pounds shrimp (uncooked, unpeeled)
1/2 cup lemon juice
salt and freshly ground pepper
1/4 teaspoon dry mustard
2 pickled jalapeños, seeded and minced
1 cup green onions, chopped with part of tops

Put 1/3 cup of the oil in a large frying pan and sauté onion and garlic over medium heat until the onion turns soft. Add shrimp, toss, and cook 4–5 minutes—or until the shrimp turns pink. Remove from heat and cool. Mix the other 1/3 cup oil with all the rest of the ingredients and add the shrimp. Marinate, covered, in the refrigerator for 24 hours, basting several times.
Serves 4–6

These are done with the shell on the shrimp, and must be peeled as they are eaten. If you wish something a little less messy, go ahead and peel and devein them before cooking—either way they make a spectacular appetizer.

Oysters Phoenix

3 dozen fresh oysters
2 tablespoons lemon juice (or lime)
1 teaspoon salt
1½ cups red onion, chopped
½ cup olive oil
1 cup white wine vinegar
1 teaspoon whole allspice
3 drops Tabasco sauce
2 cloves garlic, flattened slightly
1 pickled jalapeño, seeded and
  minced
1 teaspoon juice from the jalapeños

Shuck oysters and place with their juices in a saucepan. Add water to cover, lemon juice and salt. Simmer just until the edges of the oysters curl, 2–3 minutes, then drain immediately. Sauté onion in oil until soft and add to the oysters. Combine with all the other ingredients and let marinate, covered, in the refrigerator for 24 hours. Serve with toothpicks.
Serves 6–8

Seafood has to come a long way from the seashore to Southwestern homes, but the natives dote on it in a way coastal people, used to all that bounty, can't imagine. If you can't get oysters in the shell, the best to use for this are the small Olympias which are shipped around the country in jars.

Additional Appetizers

There are some other dishes scattered throughout the book which make admirable appetizers. Of course Guacamole is the prime example, if you are not serving it in any way with the main dish, but there are also Green Garbanzo Salad (p. 235), Green Chile Salad (p. 229), Seviche (p. 121), Rooster's Bill (p. 236), Texas Escabeche of Vegetables (p. 63), and Carne Adovada (p. 154).

Also both pumpkin seeds and toasted piñon nuts are often served with drinks in the Southwest. For cocktails you will be authentic if you serve either Margaritas, or plain tequila. Tequila is drunk in this manner: each guest holds a wedge of lime between his thumb and forefinger, and a small mound of salt in the hollow at the base of the thumb. The procedure is to taste a bit of salt, then to take a swallow of tequila, and then a taste of the lime to quench the fire.

Soups

Except for the ever popular (and misunderstood) bowl of chili, soups from the Southwest tend to be unknown to the rest of the country—though they have remarkable feast-day soups, suave avocado soups to begin any elegant meal, and many a satisfying lunch or supper dish which is cheap and easy to put together. As well, the hominy-based soup called Posole is surely one of the great dishes of the world.

Avocado Consommé

$^{1}/_{2}$ cup Monterey Jack cheese,
   grated
3 cups beef stock, heated
2 avocados, peeled, seeded, and
   sliced

Divide grated cheese among four
soup plates, then pour the hot
stock over. Garnish with avocado
slices and serve immediately.
Serves 4

A delicious simple soup to begin a meal, particularly if you have good homemade beef stock. If not, try combining canned beef bouillon with homemade chicken stock.

Chilled Avocado Soup

1 cup tomato juice
1/2 cup green onions, chopped with
    part of tops
1 clove garlic, peeled
salt and freshly ground pepper
1 whole clove
1/2 teaspoon dried basil
1/2 bay leaf
2 drops Tabasco sauce
pinch of sugar
2 tablespoons lemon juice (or lime)
3 cups light beef stock
1 avocado, peeled, seeded and
    sliced
sour cream

Place tomato juice in a saucepan and add onion, garlic, a little salt and pepper, and all the ingredients through the lemon juice. Bring to a boil, then lower heat and simmer 10 minutes. Strain the broth and put back into the pot. Add beef stock and heat to boiling. Chill thoroughly in the refrigerator. Before serving, slice avocados into soup plates, pour soup over, and garnish with sour cream.

Serves 4

A refreshing soup for summer evenings. It's nice to serve with lime wedges and crisp tortilla chips.

Avocado Cream

4 cups chicken stock (free of any
fat)
3 cups avocados, diced
¹/₄ cup lime juice (or lemon)
salt and freshly ground pepper
minced chives (or parsley or
coriander sprigs)

Place stock, avocados, and lime juice in a blender or food processor. Whirl until smooth. (This is easiest done in two batches.) Add salt and pepper to taste and chill, covered, in the refrigerator for an hour or more. Serve in chilled soup plates garnished with chives, parsley, or coriander.
Serves 6

What could be simpler? This suave soup can begin any spicy meal—served in cups rather than soup plates, it makes a welcome start to an outdoor barbecue.

Texas Gazpacho

2 cups beef stock (or canned beef
    bouillon and water)
1 cup red onion, chopped
1 green bell pepper, grated (see
    Ingredients)
6 medium tomatoes, peeled and
    chopped (or 1 large can Italian
    plum tomatoes)
1 clove garlic, minced
1/4 cup parsley, minced
2 tablespoons fresh coriander,
    minced (optional)
4 tomatillos, chopped (optional,
    see p. 275)
1/4 cup green chiles, chopped
1/2 teaspoon dried oregano
3 tablespoons lemon juice (or lime)
4 drops Tabasco sauce
pinch sugar
salt
1 tablespoon red wine
1 teaspoon lemon rind, grated
1 cup cucumber, peeled and cubed
ice cubes

Combine all ingredients except the cucumber and ice cubes. Cover and refrigerate for an hour or more. To serve, add the cucumber and ladle into cold soup plates. Add two ice cubes to each. Serve with tortilla chips.

Serves 6

This "liquid salad" is one of the best summer soups of all, whether it is encountered in Spain, Mexico, or the Southwest. Sometimes it is very simple, being no more than fresh salsa including some bell pepper and cucumber and thinned with tomato juice. This more elaborate version, encountered in San Antonio, remains a favorite, however.

Potato Soup with Green Chiles

6 green onions, chopped with part
   of tops
3 tablespoons butter
2 tablespoons flour
4 cups milk, heated
1/3 cup green chiles, chopped
3 medium potatoes, peeled and
   diced
salt
1 fresh jalapeño, seeded and
   minced (or serrano)
1 cup Monterey Jack cheese,
   grated

Sauté onions in butter in a soup pot set over medium heat. When they are soft stir in flour and cook 3–4 minutes. Add the hot milk and cook, stirring, until the soup begins to bubble. Turn heat down low, add chiles and potatoes, and salt to taste. Simmer 10 minutes, or until the potatoes are just tender. Scoop out 1 cup of the soup and purée it in a blender or food processor, then put it back in the pot. Add the jalapeño and cook 5 minutes to meld the flavors. Serve in soup plates with cheese sprinkled on top.

Serves 4

What a fine, simple, tasty supper this makes—accompanied by tortilla chips and a salad, of course.

Tomato Green Chile Soup

2 tablespoons vegetable oil
1/4 cup onion, chopped
1 clove garlic, minced
1/2 cup tomato, chopped
1/4 cup green chiles, chopped
1 1/2 cups chicken stock
1/2 cup cream
salt
2 corn tortillas
oil for frying
3/4 cup Monterey Jack cheese, cut
  in small cubes

Cook onion and garlic in oil over medium heat in a soup pot, stirring, until the onion is soft. Add tomato, chiles, and stock. Cook 20 minutes over low heat with the pot covered. Add cream, and taste for salt. Simmer another 8–10 minutes. While the soup cooks, cut edges off the tortillas so they make a square, cut the square in half, and stack the halves. Cut them into matchstick lengths. Fry in deep fat until crisp, and drain on paper towels. Salt lightly. To serve, place cheese cubes in the bottom of soup plates, ladle soup over, and top with a sprinkle of tortilla strips.

Serves 4

This is very lively-tasting for such a simple-sounding soup. It makes a satisfying lunch or supper with not much else but a glass of beer and a sound dessert.

Calabacitas Soup

1 tablespoon butter
2 cups yellow summer squash, sliced (or zucchini)
1/2 cup green onions, chopped with part of tops
1/2 cup tomato, chopped
2 cups chicken stock
1 cup cooked chicken, diced
1 cup corn (fresh, frozen, or canned)
2 tablespoons fresh coriander, minced (or 1/2 teaspoon dried oregano)
1/4 cup green chiles, chopped
salt and freshly ground pepper
1 3-ounce package cream cheese, chilled and diced

Sauté squash and onions in butter over medium heat in a large saucepan or soup pot until the onion softens. Add tomato and cook a few minutes longer. Add stock, chicken, corn, coriander or oregano, and chiles. Add salt and pepper to taste and simmer over low heat 20 minutes. Ladle into soup plates and garnish with cubes of cream cheese. Serve with hot tortillas.
Serves 4–6

Calabacitas means "squash," but, as you see, this includes the whole garden. It is particularly fine with summer produce—fresh corn scraped from the ear, tomatoes right off the vine—but it is good enough to survive the winter with small adjustments here and there.

Aztec Soup

¹/₂ cup piñon nuts
¹/₂ cup pumpkin seeds
2 tablespoons butter
¹/₂ cup onion, chopped
1 clove garlic, minced
6 cups chicken stock
2 cups yellow summer squash,
    diced (or zucchini)
2 cups corn (fresh, frozen, or
    canned)
1 avocado, peeled, seeded, and cut
    in dice
2 cups Monterey Jack cheese,
    grated
6 corn tortillas, cut in small strips
    and fried crisp

In a soup pot sauté piñon nuts and pumpkin seeds in 1 tablespoon of the butter until they are golden. Remove with a slotted spoon to paper towels. Add the other tablespoon butter and sauté onion and garlic until tender. Add stock and bring to a boil over high heat. Add squash and corn, turn heat down, and simmer 10 minutes. Serve soup in soup plates—with bowls of the piñon and pumpkin seeds, avocado cubes, cheese, and tortilla strips set out for diners to garnish the soup.

Serves 6–8

I don't know why this soup is called Aztec except perhaps because most of its ingredients are indigenous. At any rate it is a quick and easy feast for a family supper, or it makes a fine show with all the bowls of garnish to begin a company dinner.

Ranchero Bean Soup

1 pound pinto beans
1/2 pound bacon, sliced in small
  strips
1 cup tomatoes, chopped
1/4 cup green chiles, chopped
1 cup green onions, chopped with
  part of tops
1/4 cup fresh coriander, minced
salt
1/2 cup beer
lime wedges

Soak beans in plenty of water overnight, then cook them over low heat until soft (if they dry out add boiling water, not cold water, to them). Fry bacon in a saucepan over medium heat until it starts to crisp. Scoop out onto paper towels and discard all but a tablespoon of bacon fat. Add this, along with bacon, tomatoes, chiles, onions, and coriander, to the bean pot. Cook, covered, 30 minutes over low heat. Uncover, add salt to taste and enough boiling water to make the beans soupy. Simmer 10 minutes more, then add beer and heat through. Serve in bowls with lime wedges for garnish, and hot tortillas.
Serves 8–10

I dote on this hearty Texas dish. There, it would be followed by an even heartier grilled steak, with all the trimmings, but it also makes a great rib-sticking supper all on its own—with glasses of frosty beer, of course.

Pinto Bean Soup

1 tablespoon bacon fat (or
  vegetable oil)
$^{1}/_{2}$ cup onion, chopped
1 clove garlic, minced
4 cups cooked pinto beans
$^{1}/_{4}$ cup green chiles, chopped
$^{1}/_{2}$ teaspoon dried oregano
$^{1}/_{2}$ cup Cheddar cheese, grated (or
  Monterey Jack)

Melt fat in a soup pot and sauté onion and garlic in it over medium heat until soft. Add beans, chiles, and oregano. Add enough bean-cooking liquid, or water, to make the mixture soupy, and simmer 30 minutes. Add water if the mixture gets dry. Purée through a food mill, or in a food processor, and return to the pot. Add enough water to make the soup creamy, and taste for salt—it may need some if the beans weren't well-seasoned. Ladle into soup plates and sprinkle with cheese. Serve with hot tortillas.

Serves 4

A simple soup from the last of a bean pot—and it makes a fine light lunch or supper dish.

Sally's Black Bean Soup with Tortillas

3 corn tortillas
2 tablespoons olive oil (or
   vegetable oil)
1 small onion, chopped
1 clove garlic, minced
1 can black bean soup, with 1 can
   water
¼ cup green chiles, chopped
1 tablespoon fresh coriander,
   minced (optional)
1 lemon, thinly sliced

Cut tortillas in strips about 1 inch by ¼ inch. In a large saucepan, fry tortillas in oil over high heat until crisp. Remove and drain on paper towels. Sauté onion and garlic in the oil left in the pan until the onion softens. Add soup with water, chiles, coriander, and ¾ of the tortillas. Simmer 10 minutes. Garnish with lemon slices and the rest of the tortillas.
Serves 2

I'm not much a fan of canned soups, but Campbell's black bean soup is an exception—particularly as Sally Midgette enhances it here.

Puree of Garbanzo Soup

2 cups cooked garbanzos (canned
    are fine)
4 cups chicken stock
2 cups water
1/2 cup onion, chopped
1 clove garlic, minced
2 tablespoons parsley, chopped
1/4 teaspoon dried oregano
2 tablespoons butter
4 drops Tabasco sauce
salt
2 eggs
1 1/2 cups Chorizo (p. 146)
1 tablespoon vegetable oil

Place garbanzos, stock, water, onion, garlic, parsley, and oregano in a soup pot and simmer 30 minutes. Purée in a blender (the food processor won't get the soup puréed enough here) and return to the pot. If the soup seems too thick add more stock or water—it should be the consistency of thick cream. Add butter, Tabasco, and salt to taste. Beat eggs in a large bowl and gradually add the hot soup, whisking constantly. Reheat, but do not let the soup boil or the eggs will curdle. Form chorizo into small marbles and sauté until crisp in the oil. Garnish the soup with them.

Serves 6

A soup seemingly of Spanish origin that makes a simple satisfying family supper with a salad and dessert.

Meatball Soup

1 tablespoon vegetable oil
1 onion, chopped
1 cup tomatoes
4 cups water
1/4 cup green chile, chopped
1 teaspoon chili powder
1/2 teaspoon dried mint
pinch of sugar
salt
1/2 pound lean ground beef
1/2 pound lean ground pork
3/4 cup blue cornmeal (or masa
   harina)
2 eggs, beaten
1 onion, minced
1 clove garlic, minced
1/4 cup green chile, chopped
2 tablespoons fresh coriander,
   minced (or parsley)
1/4 teaspoon dried oregano
1 teaspoon salt

Cook onion in oil over medium heat in a soup pot until soft. Force the tomatoes through a sieve into the pot (or purée them in a food processor) and add water. When it comes to a boil, lower flame, and add chiles, chili powder, mint, sugar, and salt to taste. Simmer 20 minutes. Meanwhile prepare the meatballs: combine all the rest of the ingredients and shape into balls the size of a walnut. Drop them one by one into the simmering soup and cook over low heat 45 minutes more.

Serves 6

Many families in the Southwest make a similar soup for holidays, but it makes a splendid supper anytime—with hot tortillas, beer, and a dessert.

Posole

3 pounds boneless pork shoulder
3 cups chicken stock
1 onion, sliced
1 clove garlic, peeled
1/2 teaspoon dried oregano
salt
1 chicken
1 tablespoon bacon fat (or butter, or chicken fat)
2 onions, chopped
2 cloves garlic, minced
1–2 tablespoons chili powder
2 large cans (1 lb. 13 oz.) white hominy, drained
1 cup tomatoes, chopped
1 4-ounce can green chiles, chopped
1/4 cup fresh coriander, minced

The best way to make Posole is to start the day before. Put pork in a big pot with stock and enough water to cover. Add onion, garlic, oregano, and a little salt. Simmer uncovered 45 minutes, then add chicken and simmer 30 minutes more. Strain stock and refrigerate. Wrap the meats and also refrigerate. Next day, lift fat off the stock. Cut meaty parts of the pork and chicken into 1/2-inch cubes. In the same big pot sauté onion and garlic in fat until soft. Add pork and chili powder and cook several minutes, stirring. Pour in the stock—there should be 8 cups. Add hominy, tomatoes, chiles, and coriander. Simmer 20 minutes. Finally, add chicken and simmer another 15 minutes. Serve in bowls with garnishes.

Serves 8

My Posole is a composite of all that is good in the many recipes I've found over the years. It's a good deal more complex than most, but in even the simplest version Posole is one of our great regional dishes. This recipe also makes quite a large amount, but it freezes well and is wonderful to have on hand.

The garnishes for Posole should be set out in small bowls for diners to add as they wish. They should include crisp fried corn tortilla strips, diced avocados, chopped green onions, diced cream cheese, wedges of lime, sliced radishes, and shredded lettuce.

Pedernales River Chili

4 pounds beef (chuck or rump
    roast)
1 large onion, chopped
2–6 cloves garlic, minced
1 teaspoon ground cumin
1 teaspoon dried oregano
2–6 tablespoons chili powder
1 large can (28 oz.) Italian plum
    tomatoes, chopped
1 cup green chiles, chopped
2 cups water (or 1 cup beef stock,
    1 cup beer)
salt

Trim meat of fat and connective tissue, and put fat in a large frying pan. Cook over medium heat until it releases 2 tablespoons of fat, then discard the unmelted fat. Cut meat into 1/4–1/2-inch cubes. Fry it in small batches over high heat until it sears. Place all the meat back in the pan with onion and garlic, and toss another 3–4 minutes. Add cumin, oregano, chili powder, tomatoes and green chiles. Toss 3–4 minutes and add water, or stock and beer. Bring to a boil, lower heat, and simmer covered one hour. Taste for salt, then cook uncovered another hour. The meat should be tender in a rich sauce—if it seems too watery, cook down over high heat to a stew-like consistency.

Serves 6

This is a variation on President Lyndon Johnson's favorite chili. The original recipe takes advantage of so many local specialties such as "chili meat" and tomatoes canned with green chiles, unavailable in many parts of the country, that one is forced to improvise. I think it also needs the punch of more chili powder and garlic, and stock and beer rather than water. Even so, this is definitely the pure "bowl of red" as it is eaten in Texas—no beans, no nonsense. (Though sometimes venison or armadillo share the pot with Texas beef.) The Texans may be purists, but they garnish their bowl with a potpourri of hot pinto beans, shredded cheese, minced green onions, squeezes of lime juice, and the like. With steamy hot tortillas and butter, and a tossed salad, it makes one of the most typical of American meals.

Sauces and Garnishes

These are the pillars on which the whole cooking of the Southwest is raised, which make it unlike any other. I have whittled them down to ones I learned firsthand from local cooks, used day-to-day over the years, or invented myself to fill a certain niche. The sauces alone would fill a fair-sized book, if one were to list them in all their minute variations. So I don't claim that these represent any one region—they are perhaps only the flavor of my own kitchen, stretched over Arizona, New Mexico, and Texas, with edges of Colorado and California thrown in.

Red Chile Sauce

¹/₂ pound dried red chiles (New
  Mexico, Ancho, or Pasilla)
3 cups chicken stock
2 cloves garlic, peeled
2 teaspoons dried oregano
salt

Remove stems, seeds, and inner veins from the chiles. (If you have tender hands do this with rubber gloves, but even if you don't use them, remember not to rub your eyes!) When trying a chile for the first time, test one by simmering in some water 15 minutes, then taste the cooking water. If it seems bitter, use only the pulp of the chiles, putting them through a sieve and discarding the skins and cooking water. If not bitter, simmer all the chiles in water to cover for 15 minutes and purée the whole thing in a blender or food processor with the stock, garlic, and oregano. Return to the pan and simmer 15 minutes more. Taste for salt.
  Makes 3 cups

This is basic "enchilada sauce," and for those who have only tasted what comes from a can (or from restaurants outside the Southwest), it will be a revelation. This recipe makes a rather thick sauce which can be thinned with more stock or water to desired consistency. It also freezes well, so it is good to make a large amount while you're about it and then freeze it in batches. In Texas the hotness is cut by the addition of tomato sauce, which is fine if you want to go for mildness rather than brilliance. Also, you can add a little ground cumin, cloves, or allspice to give the sauce a rounder balance.

51

Quick Red Chile Sauce

2 tablespoons bacon fat (or lard, or
    vegetable oil)
2 tablespoons flour
1/2 cup red chile powder
2–3 cups chicken stock, heated
2 cloves garlic, peeled
2 teaspoons dried oregano
salt

Melt fat in a saucepan and stir in flour. Cook, stirring over medium heat, for several minutes—or until the flour turns golden. Add chile powder and stir for another minute. Add stock and stir till the sauce is smooth and thickened. Add garlic, oregano, and salt to taste. Simmer for 15 minutes. Purée in a blender or food processor.

Makes 3 cups

When you don't have chile pods this makes a fine alternative. Most Hispanic markets carry a good plain red chile in powdered form—sometimes you can find the excellent Ancho or Pasilla this way.

Green Chile Sauce

1 cup green chiles, chopped (fresh, frozen, or canned)
3/4 cup tomatillos, peeled and chopped (fresh or canned), or 1 onion, chopped
1 tablespoon butter
1 clove garlic, minced
1 tablespoon parsley, minced
1 tablespoon fresh coriander, minced (optional)
1 tablespoon flour
1/2 cup chicken stock
salt
pinch of sugar

If you are using fresh chiles char them under a broiler or over a gas flame. Put in a paper bag when they are charred all over, and steam them 10 minutes. Peel off the charred skin and remove the seeds. If you use canned tomatillos, drain them well and wash under the faucet—the juices are very acid. (You will also have to use a little more sugar later.) Heat butter in a saucepan and sauté garlic in it for a minute or two. Add chiles and tomatillo and cook over medium heat 5 minutes. Add parsley, coriander, and flour. Cook 3–4 minutes, then add stock. Stir until sauce is smooth and thickened. Add salt and sugar to taste. Cook over low heat 15–20 minutes.

Makes 2 cups

A sauce from New Mexico chef Richard Freeby, and since I first tasted it I've made it my one and only green chile sauce. It makes a splendid meal over beans, with a topping of sour cream—so good in fact you won't miss having meat. You can sauté chicken and stew in the sauce, or it can be cooked with ground beef or pork to make a filling for tacos or enchiladas. If you can't get tomatillos, substitute onions—they won't be the same, but they make a fine green chile sauce.

Chile Meat Sauce

1½ pounds ground beef
2 tablespoons bacon fat (or
    vegetable oil)
2 large onions, chopped
2 cloves garlic, minced
1½ cups canned tomatoes (or ½
    cup tomato sauce, or 4
    tablespoons tomato paste)
1 cup beef or chicken stock (or
    beer)
1 4-ounce can green chiles,
    chopped
¼ cup fresh coriander, minced
    (optional)
4 tablespoons chili powder
1 teaspoon sugar
salt
pinch of ground cloves
½ teaspoon dried oregano

Sauté beef in a large saucepan until it starts to brown. Pour any fat off and drain it on paper toweling. Add bacon fat to the pan and sauté onion and garlic over medium heat until soft. Add drained beef and all the other ingredients. Turn heat low, cover the pan, and simmer 3–4 hours, or until the sauce is dark and dense, adding more stock or beer from time to time if it gets dry. If you use a pressure cooker, it will take 1½–2 hours.

Makes 5 cups

This recipe originally came from my Aunt Alda in Gallup, New Mexico, though it has evolved a little over the twenty or more years I've been cooking it. (I also sometimes make it now with a base of red chile sauce rather than with commercial chili powder.) Its uses are endless, and I keep some frozen to have on hand all the time. It makes a superior filling for tacos or tostadas, a sauce for Cheese and Onion Enchiladas or Huevos Rancheros, or, combined with cheese, it makes Tamale Pie.

Fresh Salsa

This sauce is made so many different ways that it is almost impossible to write a comprehensive recipe for it. I play it by ear. It ought to have more or less equal proportions of chopped tomatoes and onions—fresh tomatoes and green onions are best, but canned tomatoes and yellow or red onions will do if that's what you have on hand. It needs the hotness of chiles, and again fresh roasted green chiles and minced fresh jalapeños or serranos are best, but canned green chiles and pickled jalapeños will do. Then stir in minced parsley, and fresh coriander if you have it. Last, a splash of vinegar or lime juice and salt to taste. Other ingredients to be considered are oil, oregano, garlic, tomatillos, sugar. I've even had it with rather a lot of chopped cucumber and bell pepper in it—but that's going too far, perhaps.

The range of possibilities can be covered by these two recipes. The first is from Elena, the blind California cook who produced wonderful Mexican cookbooks during the 1950s. She chops up a No. 2 can of tomatoes, an onion, and a can (unspecified) of green chiles. Then she adds a teaspoon each of coriander and oregano, 2 tablespoons wine vinegar, a tablespoon of oil, and salt and pepper to taste. She mentions that it can be varied by the addition of a can of chopped tomatillos, or a minced clove of garlic.

The second comes from one of the best of our new chefs—and one who has experimented with Southwestern foods—Jeremiah Tower. He chops 2 fresh peeled tomatoes and 2 medium red onions. Then he adds 4 large cloves of minced garlic, 2 seeded and minced serrano chiles, a whole bunch of minced coriander, and the juice of 3–4 limes. As you can imagine, this is a horse of quite a different color. If Elena's recipe needs the gumption of a little more chile and coriander, Mr. Tower's is almost bitter with too much onion and coriander. The judicious cook will find a path somewhere in between.

Jalapeño Salsa

6 pickled jalapeños, seeded and
  minced
1/2 cup green onions, chopped with
  part of tops
2 tablespoons parsley, minced
1/4 cup fresh coriander, minced
  (optional)
salt
1 tablespoon olive oil (or vegetable
  oil)
1 tablespoon lemon juice (or lime)
1/2 teaspoon Worcestershire sauce
pinch sugar

Combine all ingredients and
chill in the refrigerator for 30
minutes or so before serving.
Makes 1 cup

*I learned this sauce years ago from Frances Sommer, wife of Arizona
photographer Frederick Sommer. I've never tasted its like anywhere else, but my
table sees it constantly. It can—with the addition of some chopped tomato—be
used in place of Fresh Salsa, and it makes a glorious sauce over simple meats and
fish, but my prime use for it is over Refried Beans (first topped with a dollop of
sour cream).*

Mole Sauce

2 green bell peppers
1 teaspoon anise seeds
2 tablespoons sesame seeds
5 cloves garlic, peeled
3/4 cup almonds, blanched
3 corn tortillas, minced
6 tomatoes, peeled and chopped
   (or 1 large can Italian plum
   tomatoes)
pinch of ground cloves
1/2 teaspoon cinnamon
1 teaspoon salt
1/2 teaspoon ground coriander
2 ounces bitter chocolate, grated
2 tablespoons powdered red chile
1/2 cup vegetable oil
2 cups chicken stock (or turkey)

Grind peppers, anise, sesame, garlic, almonds, tortillas, and tomatoes in a blender or food processor. Add all the spices and chocolate and process again. Heat oil in a saucepan and add the mixture to it. Cook 3–4 minutes, then add stock and simmer 15–20 minutes. It should be thick and smooth—if necessary put back in blender or food processor to make smoother. (The sauce is better if made a day ahead, to mellow.)

Enough for 2 chickens or half a turkey breast

This ancient sauce, renowned for its use of chocolate to achieve a dark complex taste, is one of the glories of Mexican cooking, and it is hardly changed in the Southwest—for how could it be better? It is mostly restricted to cooking with chicken or turkey, but I also like to freeze any leftover in ice cube trays to have on hand as a secret addition to red chile or chile meat sauces.

Quick Mole Sauce

2 tablespoons vegetable oil
1/2 cup onion, coarsely grated
2 cloves garlic, minced
2/3 cup tomatoes, chopped
2 teaspoons chili powder
pinch of ground allspice
1 2-ounce can mole poblano
   powder
2 cups chicken stock

In a saucepan, sauté onion and garlic in oil over medium heat until soft. Add tomatoes and simmer 5 minutes. Add spices, mole powder, and chicken stock and simmer 15 minutes—or until thickened. Whirl in a blender or food processor to make a smooth sauce. Return to pan and simmer 10 minutes more.

Enough for 1 chicken

Mole powders are really quite good, but they can be livened up a little so the sauce will approach the full-scale production.

Cooked Pinto Beans

1 pound dried pinto beans (or black beans)
1 onion, chopped
1 clove garlic, peeled
3 slices bacon
2 teaspoons chili powder
1/4 cup fresh coriander, chopped (optional)

Soak beans overnight in water, or cover with water, bring to a boil, cook 5 minutes, and let sit covered an hour (this is called the quick-soak method). Bring to a boil, lower heat to a simmer, and add onion, garlic, bacon, chili powder, and coriander if you use it. Simmer several hours, adding hot water if they get too dry. When beans are tender, add salt to taste, and cook another half hour. (Timing is difficult to judge with dried beans—new crop beans take 3–4 hours, but old beans can take nearly all day. In a pressure cooker they take about 90 minutes.)
Makes 5 cups

Pinto Beans can be served as is, with a topping of Green Chile Sauce and sour cream, or turned into Refried Beans.

Refried Beans

cooked pinto beans (or black beans)
bacon fat (or lard, or vegetable oil)
sour cream
Jalapeño Salsa (p. 56)
tortilla chips

You will need about 3/4 cup of beans per serving. Heat fat in a large frying pan over medium heat—about 1 tablespoon per serving. Toss the beans in hot fat and mash them with a potato masher. Add enough bean liquid from the pot to make them creamy, lower heat, and fry until a crust forms on the bottom. If they get too dry, add some more bean liquid, and let a crust form again. Serve crust up, topped with sour cream and salsa, and with tortilla chips stuck point down in them.

Hardly a meal goes by in the Southwest without these dark rich tasty beans. It takes a little practice to get them to come out just right, but so long as you don't burn them, nothing is lost, for more liquid can be added and you can start over. I use a cast-iron frying pan for them, but a nonstick pan is fine too—for you want a pan that makes a crust without too much fat.

Lettuce and Radish Garnish

1 bunch radishes
1 tablespoon white wine vinegar
salt
1 small head iceberg lettuce

Remove leaves and stems from the radishes and grate them on the coarse side of a grater into a bowl. Add vinegar and a little salt, then let stand covered in the refrigerator for an hour or so. They should blush with pink all over and still be a bit crisp. Separate the leaves of the lettuce and stack them up. Cut in thin slivers with a sharp knife and put in a bowl of cold water to crisp. At serving time drain the lettuce and dry in a spin dryer or with paper towels. Place a mound of lettuce on the plate and top with some of the grated radishes.
Serves 4–6

This is the crisp, mild part of a Southwestern platter. For years I have tried to give it a little more sparkle, tossing the lettuce in a little vinegar and salt, trying romaine instead of iceberg, and so on. Nothing seemed right until I invented the lovely radish topping, which not only gives color, but also compliments everything else on the platter.

Parsleyed Onion Rings

1 medium white or red onion
boiling water
$1/4$ cup white wine vinegar
$1/4$ cup cold water
$1/2$ teaspoon salt
$1/2$ cup parsley, minced (or fresh
  coriander)

Peel onion and slice into thin rings. Place them in a colander and pour boiling water over them. Put in a bowl, add the rest of the ingredients, and toss. Chill covered in the refrigerator for 30 minutes or so, tossing now and again.
Serves 6

These are great on tostadas, tacos, or such dishes as El Paso Stacked Enchiladas. Or they can be used as a garnish for most any platter.

Texas Escabeche of Vegetables

3 fresh green chiles
1¹/₂ pounds carrots
2 onions
1¹/₂ cups cider vinegar
¹/₄ cup oil
2 teaspoons salt
1 tablespoon sugar
1 teaspoon dried oregano
1 bay leaf
¹/₄ teaspoon coriander seeds
¹/₄ teaspoon cumin seeds
3 whole cloves garlic, peeled
3 fresh coriander sprigs (or parsley)

Cut stems off the chiles and remove the seeds. Slice into strips about 1¹/₂ by ¹/₄ inches. Peel carrots and cut on the diagonal into ¹/₄-inch chips. Trim and peel the onions and cut them from stem to root in eighths. Put all the vegetables in a pot and add water to cover. Add all the other ingredients except garlic and coriander. Bring to a boil and cook just 1¹/₂ minutes. Remove from heat and let cool in the liquid, then divide into 3 pint jars. Tuck a clove of garlic in each, and a spring of coriander, then add enough of the liquid to cover. They can be kept in the refrigerator for a month or so, or they can be sealed in sterilized jars for further keeping.

Makes 3 pints

What a joy these crispy vegetables are to have on hand. Not only are they good as an appetizer, they also make a superb side dish with barbecued meats or an addition to tacos or tostadas.

Tortilla Specialties

Crisp or steamed, corn or flour, blue or not, those delicate flat breads called tortillas are the backbone of the Southwestern kitchen. They may become plate, fork, or hot roll at any meal. You may order them up as taco, tostada, enchilada, chimichanga, or nachos. Unexpectedly they may also thicken or stuff and garnish ordinary-seeming things. Here, they come into their own. Certainly these dishes are the ones I'd like to show in pride when such complexities are shrugged off as Tex-Mex.

Cheese and Onion Enchiladas

Dip corn tortillas in hot oil just enough to soften. (Some folks are proud to do this with their fingers, but kitchen tongs are really best.) Hold above the fat for a bit to let extra oil drip off, then dip either in hot Red Chile Sauce (p. 51) or Chile Meat Sauce (p. 54). Stack them on a plate as you cook them. Preheat oven to 350°. For each enchilada place about 1/4 cup grated Cheddar or Monterey Jack cheese along each tortilla's center, top with a good sprinkle of minced green onion, then roll them up like a crepe and place seam side down in a baking pan. Continue for all the enchiladas, sprinkling extra cheese on top when arranged. Cover with foil and heat 5–10 minutes in the oven till the cheese starts to melt. (They can also be made ahead and heated at the last minute—but don't overcook them or they will toughen.) Serve 2 per person, with more sauce poured over.

These are my basic all-purpose enchiladas. With plain Red Chile Sauce they make one of the best meatless meals known to man—served, of course, with Refried Beans, Lettuce and Radish Garnish, and so forth. Any cheese, or combination of cheeses, will work (Greek Feta and Italian Provolone are both particularly fine) but a good sharp Cheddar is hard to beat. Sliced ripe olives also make a tasty addition, both inside and out.

Stacked Green Enchiladas

1 tablespoon vegetable oil
1/2 cup green onions, minced with
   part of tops
1 clove garlic, minced
1 tablespoon parsley, minced
2 tablespoons fresh coriander,
   minced (optional)
1 small green bell pepper, grated
1/2 cup tomatillos, chopped (fresh
   or canned)
2/3 cup green chiles, chopped
salt
pinch of sugar
1 tablespoon cornstarch
1 cup milk
1 3/4 cup Monterey Jack cheese,
   grated
8 corn tortillas
oil for frying
1/2 cup piñon nuts, lightly toasted

In a saucepan, sauté onions and garlic in oil over medium heat until the onion softens. Stir in parsley, coriander, and grated green pepper. Then add tomatillos and green chiles. Simmer 8–10 minutes. Season to taste with salt and a little sugar to cut the tartness of the tomatillo. Dissolve cornstarch in milk and add to the pan. Cook slowly, stirring now and again, 10 more minutes. Remove from heat and stir in 1 cup of the cheese. Dip tortillas in hot fat until they soften, and stack them on a plate. Assemble enchiladas by placing one tortilla on a plate, topping with sauce and a sprinkle of nuts, then continuing until all are used. There should be more sauce over the top than between layers, and finally a sprinkle of the rest of the cheese. Serve cut into wedges.

Serves 4–6

These are some of the most delicious of all enchiladas—and again, completely meatless. They could be rolled up if you like, but I first had them this way and continue the practice. (Also, since they are a different shape and color they go nicely side-by-side with Cheese and Onion Enchiladas.) Cheese here should always, I think, be a creamy natural Monterey Jack, as sharper cheese is too much for their delicacy. They can also be made ahead in something like a soufflé dish the size of a tortilla, covered with foil, and then heated in a moderate oven until they are warmed through.

Sour Cream Enchiladas

Preheat oven to 350°. Dip corn tortillas in hot fat to soften. Sprinkle each with Parmesan cheese, add a dollop of sour cream, then spoon some Green Chile Sauce (p. 53) over the cream. Roll up and place seam side down in a baking dish. Bake, covered with foil, 5–10 minutes or until heated through. Serve with more of the sauce spooned over, and a bit more sour cream.

These delicate enchiladas are great to partner meats of all kinds, along with the usual beans, lettuce, and so on.

Cream Cheese Enchiladas

2 tablespoons vegetable oil
2 tablespoons green onion, minced
  with part of tops
1 green bell pepper, grated
¼ cup canned tomatoes, chopped
¼ cup juice from the tomatoes
1 3-ounce package cream cheese
6 corn tortillas
oil for frying
salt
chili powder
1 cup Monterey Jack cheese,
  grated

Sauté onion and green pepper in oil until the onion softens. Add tomatoes and their juice and simmer 10 minutes, or until the sauce thickens slightly. Add cream cheese and stir until it melts. Preheat oven to 350°. Dip tortillas in hot oil until they soften, and drain on paper toweling. Sprinkle lightly with salt and chili powder. Divide the cream cheese mixture among the tortillas and roll them up. Place seam down in a baking dish and sprinkle with jack cheese. Bake, covered with foil, 8–10 minutes or until heated through.
Makes 6 (2–3 servings)

These are very mild, of course, so they make a fine contrast to hotly spiced foods on a combination platter, or to meats such as Carne Adovada.

Avocado Enchiladas

Dip corn tortillas into hot oil to soften them, then drain on paper towels. Fill them with Guacamole (p. 219) and roll up. Serve quickly with Green Chile Sauce (p. 53) or Fresh Salsa (p. 55).

These have a fine flavor, but they should be handled quickly so the tortillas stay hot and the guacamole begins to melt in them slightly. They are particularly nice with eggs.

Rolled Bean Enchiladas

Dip corn tortillas in hot oil until just softened and drain on paper towels. (Or, if you have some on hand, fry lightly in bacon fat—this gives them a wonderful flavor.) Dip tortillas in liquid from the pinto bean pot, and roll up with a filling of beans, a little minced pickled jalapeño, some chopped green onion, and some grated cheese—Jack or Cheddar. Spoon some more of the bean liquid over them, salt lightly, and sprinkle some chili powder over the top. Heat in a moderate oven, covered with foil, 8–10 minutes or until the cheese begins to melt.

I think of bean enchiladas essentially as a way to use up ingredients after a meal, and make them for myself for lunch, or serve them up as a humble supper with Lettuce and Radish Garnish (p. 61) and a substantial dessert.

Stacked Bean Enchiladas

10 corn tortillas
oil for frying
2 cups cooked pinto beans
3 pickled jalapeño peppers, seeded
  and minced
3 tablespoons fresh coriander,
  minced (optional)
1 cup cream
salt
minced green onions

Preheat oven to 350°. Dip tortillas in hot oil to soften, and drain on paper towels. Combine beans, peppers, and coriander. Lightly salt the cream to taste. Make layers in a soufflé dish, starting and ending with a tortilla. Pour cream over the stack and bake uncovered for 15–20 minutes, or until the cream is absorbed. Serve sliced into wedges, and sprinkled with green onions.
  Serves 4

Another dish for a simple family supper—creamy, substantial, and tasty.

El Paso Stacked Enchiladas

1 cup green chiles, chopped
1 cup canned tomatoes, chopped
1 cup cream
1 cup mild Cheddar cheese, grated
1/2 cup sour cream
salt
6 corn tortillas
oil for frying
1 cup mild Cheddar cheese, grated
Parsleyed Onion Rings (p. 62)

Put chiles and tomatoes (with all the can juices) in a saucepan and simmer 30 minutes, or until all the juice is absorbed. Stir in cream and cheese just until the cheese melts (it shouldn't boil). Then stir in sour cream and salt to taste and remove from the fire. Preheat oven to 350°. Run tortillas through a little hot oil until they soften, and dip each into the sauce as you go. Place them on a plate. Layer the tortillas in a soufflé dish about their diameter, first a tortilla, then some sauce, a sprinkle of cheese, then another tortilla, and so on. Bake 15–20 minutes, or until bubbly. Cut in 6 wedges, and serve with the onion rings on top.
Serves 3–6

These creamy mild enchiladas are great to serve when the other dishes are hot and spicy. They make a fine brunch dish with scrambled eggs.

Texas Turkey Enchilada Casserole

3 dried red chiles, stemmed and
    seeded
1 cup milk
1 tablespoon butter
1/2 cup onion, chopped
1 clove garlic, minced
6 fresh mushrooms, thinly sliced
1/2 cup tomatoes, chopped
1/4 teaspoon dried oregano (or
    marjoram)
cream
salt
4 corn tortillas
oil for frying
1 1/2–2 cups cooked turkey,
    chopped (or chicken)
1 cup Monterey Jack cheese,
    grated (or mild Cheddar)

Preheat oven to 350°. Place prepared chiles in a saucepan with milk. Bring to a boil, lower heat, cover the pan, and simmer 15 minutes. Place in a blender or food processor, and purée the chiles thoroughly. Melt butter in a saucepan over medium heat. Add onion and garlic, and cook a few minutes. Stir in mushrooms and cook another few minutes, then add tomatoes and oregano. Let mixture cook over low heat 10 minutes, then scrape the chile paste in. Add cream and salt to taste. Simmer 10–15 minutes, then remove from fire. Run tortillas through hot oil until they soften. Dip into the sauce and lay on a plate. Put one tortilla in the bottom of a soufflé dish about the diameter of the tortillas. Sprinkle with some turkey, then cheese, then some sauce. Repeat layers, ending with enough sauce to cover the tortilla completely, and a sprinkle of cheese. Bake 20–25 minutes or until heated through and beginning to bubble. Serve in wedges.

Serves 4–6

Creamy and delightful, and not terribly hot. These are a fine way to use up leftover turkey, or the last of a baked chicken.

Pork Enchiladas

8 corn tortillas
oil for frying
¼ cup Chorizo (p. 146)
½ cup onion, chopped
1 cup roast pork, shredded (or
    Carnitas, p. 144)
2 tablespoons fresh coriander,
    minced (or parsley)
1 pickled jalapeño pepper, seeded
    and minced
½ cup Monterey Jack cheese,
    grated
½ green bell pepper, grated (see
    p. 273)
½ cup onion, grated
1 teaspoon chili powder
pinch each of ground coriander,
    nutmeg, cloves, cinnamon,
    thyme and black pepper
salt
½ cup Monterey Jack cheese,
    grated
green olives, sliced

Preheat oven to 350°. Dip tortillas in hot oil until they soften; drain on paper towels. Stir chorizo in a frying pan over medium heat until it crumbles and releases fat. Add onion and cook until it softens. Add pork, coriander or parsley, and jalapeño. Cook several minutes more. (The chorizo should give plenty of fat, but if not, you can add a little.) Remove mixture from the pan with a slotted spoon and place in a bowl. Stir in cheese. In the fat left in the pan, fry grated pepper and onion for several minutes. Add spices and cook a few minutes more. Taste for salt. Roll pork mixture in tortillas and place seam down in a baking dish. Spread the onion–green pepper mixture over, then sprinkle with cheese and decorate with sliced olives. Bake, covered, 10–15 minutes or until warmed through and beginning to bubble.

Makes 8

These aren't particularly hot, but they are rich and spicy. They make an excellent addition to any combination platter.

Chicken Mole Enchiladas

1/2 cup onion, chopped
1 tablespoon vegetable oil
1/2 cup tomatoes, chopped
1/4 cup blanched almonds
1 tablespoon raisins
6 green pimiento-stuffed olives
1 cup cooked chicken, diced
6 corn tortillas
oil for frying
1/2 recipe Mole Sauce (p. 57, 58)

Preheat oven to 350°. Sauté onion in oil until soft. Add tomatoes and simmer 5 minutes. Chop almonds, raisins, and olives fine and add to the tomato-onion mixture. Simmer a few minutes, then add the chicken and keep warm. Dip tortillas in hot oil until they soften. Drain on paper towels. Dip tortillas in hot mole sauce and place on a plate. Divide the filling among them, roll up, and place seam down in a baking dish. Heat, covered with foil, about 10 minutes—or until warmed through.
Makes 6

These are also a fine addition to any platter. I like to sprinkle them with lightly toasted sesame seeds and garnish with radish slices.

Aztec Pie

5 corn tortillas
2 3-ounce packages of cream
cheese, at room temperature
1 4-ounce can green chiles
²/₃ cup cream
1 teaspoon salt

Preheat oven to 350°. Spread 4 tortillas with the cheese. Purée chiles in a blender or food processor. Place one cheese-spread tortilla in the bottom of a soufflé dish the size of a tortilla, spread it with some of the chile purée, then continue making layers, placing the extra tortilla on top. Mix cream with salt and pour over. Bake, covered with foil, for 20 minutes or until all the cream is absorbed. Serve in wedges.

Serves 4

I use this mild and sensuous dish constantly on combination platters, as a foil for all the color and spice and sauces.

Chicken (or Turkey) and Green Chile Pie

6 corn tortillas
oil for frying
Chicken with Green Chiles and
  Sour Cream (p. 136)
1 cup Monterey Jack cheese,
  grated

Preheat oven to 350°. Dip tortillas in hot oil until softened, then drain on paper towels. Place 1 tortilla in the bottom of a soufflé dish, top with some of the chicken mixture, then sprinkle with cheese. Continue making layers—ending with a tortilla and cheese. Bake, covered with foil, 20–30 minutes—or until starting to bubble. Serve cut in wedges.
Serves 4

A wonderful way to use up leftover chicken or turkey, and a dish good enough for company.

Burritos

Burritos are made from large flour tortillas, steamed to soften, then wrapped quickly around a warm filling. They are—with tacos—about the best sandwich ever devised. Restaurants have a perfect device to steam the tortillas, but at home one must make do. If they are very fresh they can be quickly passed over a hot griddle until they puff slightly, but the best general method, I think, is to wrap them in foil and let them warm up in the oven. A filling is piled near the center of the warm tortilla, fresh salsa is ladled over the filling, then you fold a flap over the filling, tuck in the sides to make an envelope, and roll them to seal. If they are to be eaten by hand it is nice to wrap them in foil, which can be stripped away as you eat while still holding the whole thing together.

Of course, like any sandwich, burritos may be filled with anything: beans, meat, rice, cheese, guacamole. Sometimes the salsa is spooned over the outside, rather than tucked in, and sometimes guacamole is slathered over. They are all good, but these are some of my favorites:

1. Carnitas (p. 144), Pinto Beans, Fresh Salsa (p. 55)
2. Carne Asada (p. 177), Pinto Beans, Cheese, Fresh Salsa
3. Carne Adovada (p. 154), Guacamole (p. 219)
4. Pinto Beans, chopped green onions, grated cheese

Chimichangas

These are simply burritos deep fried, and they can be assembled with any filling you'd put in a burrito. Since one doesn't have to work so quickly to maintain a warm dish, they are more suitable to make at home for a combination platter than are burritos. For this reason the salsa is usually omitted from the filling and then later spooned over the chimichanga.

After you have rolled up the flour tortilla fix it with toothpicks. Heat oil to about 375° in a deep fat fryer, then fry one at a time for about a minute and a half, turning to brown both sides. Drain on paper towels and serve with Fresh Salsa (p. 55), Guacamole (p. 219), sour cream, or Red Chile Sauce (p. 51).

Bean Chimichangas

1¹/₃ cups Refried Beans (p. 60)
1 cup Monterey Jack or Cheddar, grated
4 flour tortillas
oil for frying
¹/₂ cup Monterey Jack or Cheddar, grated
sour cream
Fresh Salsa (p. 55)

Heat beans in a frying pan and stir cheese in until it melts. Divide between the tortillas and roll them up, tucking in ends as you roll. Fasten with toothpicks. Fry in hot oil (375°) for 2–3 minutes, or until they are golden brown on all sides. Lift out and drain on paper towels. Place in a baking pan, sprinkle the rest of the cheese over, then put under a broiler until the cheese melts. Serve with a dollop of sour cream on top, and the salsa.

Makes 4

Another delight for vegetarians—and the rest of us too.

Everyday Tostadas

corn tortillas
oil for frying
pinto beans, warmed
Chile Meat Sauce (p. 54), warmed
   (or Carnitas [p. 144], Carne
   Asada [p. 177], Carne Adovada
   [p. 154], Tinga [p. 145])
grated cheese
sour cream
shredded lettuce
sliced radishes
Parsleyed Onion Rings (p. 62)
   (optional)
Fresh Salsa (p. 55) (or Jalapeño
   Salsa [p. 56])

Fry tortillas one at a time in hot oil using kitchen tongs to hold them down in the oil (only about 1 inch of oil is necessary). Hold the tongs slightly spread in the middle of the tortillas so the edges puff up around and form a slight cup shape. As they start to crisp, turn them over to make sure they crisp evenly, then lift out and place on paper towels to drain. It's good to make these a little ahead and keep them in a warm oven— that way if one or so isn't thoroughly crisp they have a chance to dry out. Have beans and whatever meat you choose in chafing dishes, and place all other ingredients in separate bowls. Guests (or family) should assemble their own tostadas roughly in the order given above, using the tortillas as a base. They are, of course, eaten by hand rather than with a fork and knife. (Over a plate and with plenty of napkins!)

Tostadas are my favorite way to use up all the things I've already prepared for a Southwestern meal. For family, the beans and meat can just sit in the warm pots on the stove, and people can go to the kitchen to assemble their own heaps. But party guests like to heap them up too from chafing dishes and pretty bowls—anyway, fearless party guests do.

Cynthia's Tostadas with Sour Cream

8 corn tortillas
oil for frying
2 cups Refried Beans (p. 60)
1/2 can undiluted black bean soup
  (Campbell's)
1 pint sour cream
1 4-ounce can green chiles,
  chopped
grated Parmesan cheese

Fry tortillas in hot oil as in Everyday Tostadas (p. 86). Drain on paper towels, and keep warm in the oven. Heat refried beans and the soup in a saucepan and combine sour cream and chiles in a bowl. To assemble, spread bean paste over the tortillas, top with a spoonful of sour cream, and sprinkle with Parmesan.
Makes 8

I don't know what makes these so spectacularly good, but they are. They make a fine quick lunch, or supper with soup of some sort, and I have even turned them out as appetizers.

Chorizo Tostadas

6 corn tortillas
oil for frying
$^1/_2$ cup Chorizo (p. 146)
1 tablespoon vegetable oil
$^1/_2$ cup canned tomatoes, chopped
$^1/_4$ cup juice from the can
$^1/_3$ cup green chiles, chopped
1 3-ounce package cream cheese
shredded lettuce
salt
vinegar
6 green onions, minced with part
   of tops

Fry tortillas as in Everyday Tostadas (p. 86), and drain on paper towels. Keep warm in the oven. Put chorizo in a frying pan and stir over medium high heat until it is crumbly and begins to crisp. Remove with a slotted spoon to paper towels to drain off fat. Wipe out the pan and add oil. Add tomatoes, juice, and chiles and cook a few minutes. Then stir in the cream cheese. Stir until the cheese melts, and remove from heat. To assemble, place some lettuce on each tortilla, then some of the chorizo with a sprinkle of salt and vinegar. Top with the tomato mixture and green onions.
Makes 6

These make an almost perfect tostada thanks to all the contrasts in texture and flavor.

Carne Adovada Tostadas

4 corn tortillas
oil for frying
2 avocados, peeled and seeded
2 tablespoons green onion, minced
1 tablespoon lemon juice
salt
2 cups Carne Adovada (p. 154)
1 cup Monterey Jack cheese,
  grated
sour cream
Lettuce and Radish Garnish (p. 61)

Fry tortillas as in Everyday Tostadas (p. 86), drain on paper towels, and keep warm in the oven. Mash avocados and combine with onion, lemon juice, and salt to taste. Spread the tortillas with the avocado mixture, top with hot Carne Adovada, sprinkle with cheese, and finish with some sour cream and Lettuce and Radish Garnish.
Makes 4

A delicious tostada that softens the fiery meat with mild avocado, cheese, and cream.

Tostadas with Beans and Chorizo

4 corn tortillas
oil for frying
2 cups Refried Beans (p. 60),
   heated
^{1}/$_2$ cup Chorizo (p. 146)
1 cup Cheddar cheese, grated
Parsleyed Onion Rings (p. 62)
sliced radishes

Fry tortillas as in Everyday Tostadas (p. 86), drain on paper towels, and keep warm in the oven. Heat beans. Fry chorizo in a dry frying pan set over medium high heat, stirring to crumble it. When it begins to brown, scoop out and drain on paper towels, then stir into the beans. Divide the bean mixture over tortillas, and top with cheese, onion rings, and radishes.

Makes 4

A very snappy tostada with lots of character. It makes a fine lunch or supper dish.

Squash Flower Tostadas

4 corn tortillas
oil for frying
2 tablespoons olive oil
2 cloves garlic, peeled and slightly
    flattened
12 squash flowers, slightly
    flattened
$^1/_2$ cup green onion, minced with
    part of tops
salt and freshly ground pepper
4 ounces cream cheese, at room
    temperature

Fry tortillas as in Everyday Tostadas (p. 86), drain on paper towels, and keep warm in the oven. In a frying pan, sauté the garlic cloves in olive oil over medium heat. When they turn golden remove from the pan and sauté the flowers in the oil a minute or two per side. Add onion, lower heat, and cook until the onion softens. Spread cream cheese on the tortillas, and top with the squash flowers.
Makes 4

Another recipe for squash flowers for those who have a garden. I like to serve them with soup, either for lunch or at the beginning of a fine dinner.

Cheese Tostadas with Flour Tortillas

Place flour tortillas under a medium broiler flame. When they begin to puff up a bit, brush with melted butter, and as they start to brown, sprinkle with grated sharp Cheddar. Serve quickly when the cheese is melted, topped with Fresh Salsa (p. 55).

Tostadas made with flour tortillas become a very different thing—they are usually conceived of as a snack food, quickly turned out and quickly eaten.

Flour Tostadas with Chile Meat Sauce

Prepare tortillas as in the preceding recipe, but spread them with
warm Chile Meat Sauce (p. 54) and a sprinkle of grated Monterey Jack
or Cheddar before the final broiling. Sprinkle with Jalapeño Salsa (p. 56)
and Lettuce and Radish Garnish (p. 61).

*These make a more substantial and fiery dish than the preceding tostadas, and
are suitable for a lunch or supper.*

Everyday Tacos

corn tortillas
oil for frying
Chile Meat Sauce (p. 54), warmed
   (or Carnitas [p. 144], Carne
   Asada [p. 177], Carne Adovada
   [p. 154], Tinga [p. 145])
pinto beans, warmed
grated cheese
tomatoes, chopped (optional)
avocados, chopped (optional)
sour cream
shredded lettuce
Fresh Salsa (p. 55)

Fry tortillas in an inch or more of hot oil. While they are still pliable grasp them on one side with kitchen tongs and fold one half over the other—not too tightly as there should be an opening of about 2 inches between the two halves at the top. Turn as the tortillas crisp to make sure they are done on both sides and at the fold in the bottom. (It may be necessary to insert tongs in the middle to keep them from closing up—in essence you want a crisp U-shaped cup.) Drain on paper towels, and keep warm in the oven. Fill taco shells with the remaining ingredients, in about the above order. Have a bowl of salsa for diners to spoon more on if they wish.

Tacos are really anything a tostada can be, but in another shape. They sound a little tricky to cook, and there are even metal "shells" that they can be fried in, but once you get the hang of it they go very easily and quickly. Practically any of the tostada recipes can be used for filling them.

Chicken Tacos with Green Chile Sauce

6 corn tortillas
oil for frying
1 3-ounce package of cream cheese, at room temperature
¼ cup green onions, minced with part of tops
1 tablespoon lemon juice (or lime)
pinch of dried oregano
1 cup cooked chicken, diced (or turkey)
salt
2 avocados, peeled, seeded and diced
Green Chile Sauce (p. 53)
shredded lettuce

Cook tortillas as in Everyday Tacos (p. 95). Drain on paper towels, and keep warm in the oven. Cream the cheese in a bowl, and stir in onions, lemon juice, oregano, chicken, and salt to taste. Place this mixture in the bottom of the tortillas, top with avocados, warm sauce, and sprinkle with lettuce.

Makes 6

A particularly pleasing taco in its contrasts of taste and texture.

Quesadillas

These need very fresh tortillas—either corn or flour—so they will be soft enough to fold over and fasten with toothpicks without breaking. If they don't seem soft and pliable, wrap them in a towel and steam in a colander set over simmering water for 5 minutes or so. The simplest and most common quesadilla consists of merely a slice of cheese placed over half the tortilla, which is then folded over, fastened with toothpicks, and fried in hot oil (about 360°) for only a minute or two to brown and crisp the tortilla and melt the cheese. Or, it can be brushed with butter and baked in a 350° oven until sightly crisp. Baking is particularly fine with flour tortillas.

Quesadillas can be eaten out of hand like a sandwich, for a snack, with some Fresh Salsa (p. 55) to dip them in, or they can be served as a hearty appetizer. They are delicious with just cheese, but they can have any filling. These are some fine variations:
1. Monterey Jack cheese, and Green Chile Sauce (p. 53)
2. Picadillo (p. 153) and cream cheese
3. Squash flowers, green chile, and grated cheese

Eggs

Southwestern egg dishes are so interesting there is no reason to save them for breakfast alone. You can turn to these for lunch or late supper acclaim any time, one after the other. I do, anyway. Everyone knows Huevos Rancheros in one form or another, but few have eaten the lovely Tortas de Huevos made with blue cornmeal, or a Green Chilaquiles omelet.

Huevos Rancheros

2 cups Red Chile Sauce (p. 51) (or
  Chile Meat Sauce [p. 54], or
  Green Chile Sauce [p. 53])
8 eggs
8 corn tortillas
oil for frying
2 cups Monterey Jack cheese,
  grated (or Cheddar)

Heat sauce of your choice in a saucepan. Gently fry or poach eggs in your favorite manner. Pass tortillas through hot oil to soften them. Place two tortillas on each plate, top each with an egg, then ladle sauce all around them (not covering the yolk). Sprinkle cheese over and serve. The plates can be assembled and placed in a warm oven to melt the cheese, if need be.

Serves 4

The classic egg dish both of Mexico and the Southwestern United States, and surely it remains one of the best ways ever devised to consume eggs. Any of the sauces are good here, though restaurants usually only present them with Red Chile Sauce. They can also be sprinkled with minced green onion, or garnished with avocado. A heartier variation spreads the tortillas with Refried Beans, tops the eggs with Green Chile Sauce, and garnishes the plate with sliced avocado.

Tortas de Huevos

4 eggs, separated
2 tablespoons blue cornmeal (or
    fine stone-ground cornmeal)
salt
oil for frying
2 cups Red Chile Sauce (p. 51)

Beat whites stiff, but not dry. Whisk yolks in another bowl and fold them with cornmeal and salt to taste into the whites. Heat ½ inch oil in a frying pan and drop the egg mixture in by large spoonsful. They will puff up and turn pale gold, and need to cook only about half a minute per side. Lift them out with a slotted spoon; drain on paper towels. They will settle into flatter shapes, but will puff up again as they cook in sauce. Put sauce in a frying pan large enough to hold all the tortas, and thin it with water if necessary—it shouldn't be thicker than cream. Put the tortas in, cover the pan, and let them steam over low heat 5 minutes. Serve on warm plates in a puddle of sauce.
    Serves 4

Felice Gonzales cooked these for me first in Albuquerque, after quizzing her grandmother about the exact process. I've been cooking them ever since, for they are delightful as a quick and inexpensive meal any time of day or night. I usually sprinkle them with a little cheese, and partner them with Lettuce and Radish Garnish (p. 61) and Refried Beans (p. 60).

Eggs *with* Stuffed Green Chiles

4 whole green chiles (freshly
    prepared, or canned)
1 cup Monterey Jack cheese,
    grated (or Cheddar)
2 tablespoons butter
2 tablespoons vegetable oil
4 eggs, beaten
salt
1/4 cup Parmesan cheese, grated

Slit the sides of the chiles and stuff with cheese. Press edges together. Melt butter and oil in an 8-inch frying pan, tilting it so the sides are coated. Place chiles in the pan and cook over medium heat until the cheese starts to melt—3 or 4 minutes. Beat eggs with a little salt and pour over the chiles. Cook as you would an omelet, lifting the edges so the uncooked egg can run underneath. When the eggs are set, separate the chiles into serving portions and lift out onto plates. Sprinkle with Parmesan.
    Serves 2

As well as a breakfast dish this makes a succulent lunch or supper, with Refried Beans (p. 60) and hot corn tortillas slathered with butter.

Green Chilaquiles Omelet

per person:

1 corn tortilla
oil for frying
salt
ground cumin
2 eggs
$^1/_2$ cup Green Chile Sauce (p. 53),
   heated
$^1/_2$ cup Monterey Jack cheese,
   grated (or Cheddar)
1 tablespoon butter

Cut the tortilla's round edges off so you have a square. Cut the square in half, stack the halves, and cut into matchstick strips. Fry in hot oil until crisp, drain on paper towels, and sprinkle with salt and a little cumin immediately. Beat eggs in a bowl with a little salt, and have sauce and cheese ready. Melt butter in a 6-inch omelet pan over medium heat. When it sizzles pour the eggs in. When they start to set, lift edges with a fork to let unset egg run under, then spread with sauce. Keep lifting the edges to let any runny egg under, but don't let the omelet overcook—the edges should be set, but the top should still be a little undercooked. Remove from the heat, sprinkle with tortilla strips, and then cheese. Run under a broiler for a minute or so to melt the cheese, then slip face up onto a plate.

These beauties can be made in relays and kept warm in the oven, or you can make a double recipe in an 8-inch omelet pan and cut the omelet in quarters to serve. They look very pretty garnished with tomato quarters and a sprig of fresh coriander.

Shirred Eggs in Green Chile Cups

butter
4 whole green chiles (freshly
  prepared, or canned)
4 eggs
salt
1/4 cup sour cream

Preheat oven to 350°. Lightly butter 4 custard cups and line each with a green chile. Break an egg into each and salt lightly. Beat sour cream till it softens and dribble over the eggs. Bake 8–10 minutes, or until the tops of the yolks start to set.

Serves 4

A simple dish with a lively flavor. You might, if you wished, sprinkle a little grated Parmesan over them, but they really don't need anything.

Eggs *in Spanish Sauce*

1 green bell pepper, grated
½ cup onion, minced
1 clove garlic, minced
1 tablespoon olive oil (or vegetable oil)
1 cup canned tomato sauce
1 tablespoon parsley, minced (or fresh coriander)
1 teaspoon chili powder
6 eggs
salt
1 cup Monterey Jack cheese, grated

Preheat oven to 400°. Sauté pepper, onion, and garlic in oil for 5 minutes over medium heat. Add tomato sauce, parsley, chili powder and salt. Cook over low heat 10–15 minutes. Place in a shallow casserole large enough to hold all the eggs. Break eggs over, salt lightly, then scatter cheese over the whites of the eggs. Bake 5 minutes or just until the whites are firm.
Serves 3

A fine breakfast dish served with hot steamed tortillas with butter to slather over them, perhaps some bacon or fried chorizo patties, and coffee.

Eggs Baked with Beans

1 tablespoon vegetable oil
1/2 cup onion, chopped
2 cloves garlic, minced
1 cup tomatoes, chopped
2 cups Refried Beans (p. 60)
4 eggs
1 cup Cheddar cheese, grated

Preheat oven to 325°. In a saucepan, cook onion and garlic in oil over medium heat until the onion softens. Add tomatoes, turn heat low, and simmer for 15 minutes. Stir in the beans and cook until the mixture heats through. Lightly grease an 8-inch-square baking dish. Spread bean mixture in it. Break eggs over—one per corner—then sprinkle with cheese. Cover with foil and bake 10–15 minutes, or until eggs are set as you like them. (10 minutes will make them just cooked, and 15 will set them solidly.) Serve at once.

Serves 4

This sounds a little strange but it is very good indeed, and makes a fine light brunch or supper with Lettuce and Radish Garnish and Tortilla Chips. When cooking it, taste the bean-tomato mixture. Depending on the seasoning of the beans, you might want a little salt—and if you have some green chile on hand, that won't hurt either.

Scrambled Eggs with Tortillas

3 tablespoons butter
4 green onions, minced with part
of tops
1/2 cup tomatoes, chopped
(optional)
1 tablespoon parsley, minced (or
fresh coriander)
12 corn tortillas, cut in 1/2 × 1 1/2-
inch strips
6 eggs, beaten
1/4 cup green chiles, chopped
salt and freshly ground pepper
Parmesan cheese, grated

Melt butter in a good size frying pan and add onions, tomatoes, and parsley. Cook over low heat 5 minutes. Turn heat up and add tortillas. Fry, stirring constantly, until they start to crisp just slightly. Then lower heat and stir in eggs, green chile, and salt and pepper to taste. Keep lifting the mixture off the bottom of the pan until the eggs set. Place on warm plates and sprinkle with cheese.

Serves 4

Variations on this dish exist all over the Southwest, but this is my favorite. There is something about all those tortillas that make eggs really sit up. It is a little unlovely looking, so the cheese is necessary for camouflage (Monterey Jack is good here too) and a few sprigs of parsley or coriander don't hurt. I like it as a simple supper with a tossed salad and fruit for dessert.

Scrambled Eggs with Chorizo

¹/₂ cup Chorizo (p. 146)
4 corn tortillas
oil for frying
2 tablespoons butter
8 eggs, beaten
salt and freshly ground pepper
sour cream
4 green onions, minced with part
   of tops

Cook chorizo in a dry frying pan over medium heat 15–20 minutes, stirring with a fork to crumble. It will be done when browned. Drain on paper towels and keep warm. Pass tortillas through hot oil just to soften them. Place the tortillas on plates and keep warm also. Heat butter in a saucepan (or the same frying pan, wiped out) and scramble eggs with salt and pepper to taste. They should be soft and creamy. Top each tortilla with eggs, then chorizo, then a dollop of sour cream. Sprinkle with onions and serve.

Serves 4

This is much more fun than scrambled eggs, sausage patties, and toast. Try it some sunny morning when you have a little chorizo on hand.

Green Chile Soufflé in a Tortilla Crust

7 corn tortillas
oil for frying
1 cup Green Chile Sauce (p. 53)
4 eggs, separated
1 tablespoon flour
1³/₄ cups Monterey Jack cheese,
   grated
¹/₂ cup green chiles, chopped

Preheat oven to 375°. You will need a 7- or 8-inch casserole for this dish—I use a 7-inch cast-iron frying pan, which works fine. Pass tortillas through hot oil to soften, then dip each into sauce. Place one in the center of a lightly oiled casserole and arrange the rest of them overlapping around the sides and the center tortilla. Beat egg whites stiff, but not dry, then beat yolks with flour. Fold this, 1 cup of the cheese, and the green chiles into the whites. Pour into the tortilla-lined casserole, and fold the tortillas over the filling. Top with the sauce, and sprinkle with the rest of the cheese. Bake, uncovered, 30 minutes—or until puffed and crisping around the edges. Serve cut into wedges.
   Serves 4

An unusual and very attractive dish, with slightly crisp yet chewy tortillas cupping a fine soufflé. It makes an excellent brunch or supper dish, garnished with tomato quarters and a sprig of parsley.

Fish

Though only Texas has a coast for seafood, the other Southwestern states have good fishing in mountain streams and dammed lakes. And when fresh caught, of course the Southwestern cook prepares fish simply as any—grilled over mesquite with a squeeze of lime, or quickly sautéed with fresh coriander butter. They also have ways with frozen produce that are chock full of spice and chile and general sass.

Fish Fillets with Parsley and Piñon Sauce

¹/₄ cup olive oil
¹/₂ cup piñon nuts, chopped
¹/₂ cup parsley, minced (or fresh
  coriander)
2 tablespoons lemon juice (or lime)
1 pickled jalapeño, seeded and
  minced
salt
4 serving portions fish fillets
flour
salt and freshly ground pepper
1 tablespoon butter
2 tablespoons vegetable oil

Use a little of the olive oil to sauté the piñon nuts in a saucepan until lightly golden. Mix nuts with the rest of the oil, parsley, lemon, jalapeño, and salt to taste. Flour fish and salt and pepper lightly. Heat butter and oil in a frying pan, and sauté the fillets over high heat, quickly browning them on both sides. Serve with sauce poured over.

Serves 4

This sprightly dish can be adapted to any type of fish fillet available. Only remember that these vary from thin slices of sole to thicker fillets of snapper and other fish. A good rule to remember is James Beard's: whatever method of cooking, fish should be cooked 10 minutes per inch of thickness. This means if your fillet is ¹/₂ inch thick it will need a total of 5 minutes, and so on.

Swordfish Steaks with Green Chile Sauce

4 swordfish steaks
2 tablespoons lemon juice (or lime)
salt
2 cups Green Chile Sauce (p. 53)
parsley sprigs, or fresh coriander

Sprinkle fish with lemon juice and a little salt. Heat sauce in a frying pan large enough to hold all the steaks. Place fish in the sauce, cover, and simmer about 10 minutes, or until the fish whitens and flakes easily. Lift fish out onto warm plates, bring the sauce to a good boil, then pour over the fish and serve with parsley or fresh coriander garnish.
Serves 4

This is what they do in New Mexico to a good, thick portion of fish— swordfish here, but it could be a red snapper fillet. It is not suitable for delicate textured fish, however. Serve it with Rice with Toasted Piñon Nuts (p. 206).

Red Snapper with Chile Orange Sauce

6 serving portions red snapper
   fillets
3 tablespoons olive oil (or
   vegetable oil)
1 cup onion, chopped
2 cloves garlic, minced
1/2 cup canned tomato sauce
1 teaspoon chili powder
1/2 teaspoon dried oregano
1/4 teaspoon ground cumin
juice of 1 orange
salt and freshly ground pepper
1 orange, peeled and sliced

Preheat oven to 350°. Fry fish lightly in oil, then remove from pan and sauté onion and garlic in the same oil until onion softens. Add tomato sauce, chili powder, oregano, and cumin. Simmer 15 minutes, or until sauce begins to thicken. Remove from heat and stir in orange juice, and salt and pepper to taste. Take a shallow casserole large enough to hold all the fish in one layer, and oil it generously. Place fish in, pour sauce over, and top each piece of fish with an orange slice. Bake 20–30 minutes, or until bubbly.

Serves 6

A Mexican-influenced dish which can be used for any firm-fleshed fish. Serve it with Rice with Toasted Piñon Nuts (p. 206) and a white wine.

Fish Casserole with Chile and Wine

1 clove garlic, minced
1/2 teaspoon ground cumin
2 teaspoons chili powder
3 tablespoons olive oil (or
  vegetable oil)
6 serving portions fish fillets or
  steaks
1 green bell pepper, chopped
1/2 cup tomatoes, chopped
1 cup red wine
salt
pinch of sugar
6 drops Tabasco sauce
3 tablespoons olive oil (or
  vegetable oil)
1/2 teaspoon dried oregano
2 tablespoons parsley, minced (or
  fresh coriander)
12 green olives
24 capers

Mix garlic with cumin and chili powder in a small bowl until it makes a paste. Heat oil in a frying pan and quickly fry fish—only a minute or so on each side is enough. Remove to a platter and fry pepper in the same oil for 5 minutes. Add garlic paste and tomatoes and cook another 5 minutes. Add wine and simmer a few minutes more, then add salt to taste, sugar, and Tabasco. Place fish in a shallow casserole, layered with a mixture of the tomato sauce, olive oil, oregano, parsley, olives, and capers. The top layer should be of the liquid. Ths is best if covered and kept overnight in the refrigerator before cooking, but it can be kept for only 4–5 hours if you prepare it in the middle of the day for dinner that evening. It should be brought to room temperature before serving. Shortly before serving, heat in a 350° oven for 15–20 minutes, or until it starts to bubble.

Serves 6

You certainly wouldn't want to use delicate sole or flounder here, but the recipe is fine for coarser types of fish such as red snapper, haddock, cod, or swordfish. The red wine lends an unusual note for a fish dish and seems to balance all the spices, chiles, olives, and capers. It makes a good company meal with Guacamole Rice Ring (p. 208).

Orange Snapper

4 red snapper fillets (or other fish)
$^1/_2$ cup green onions, minced with
  part of tops
1 pickled jalapeño, seeded and
  minced
grated peel and juice from 1 large
  orange
salt
4 orange slices

Marinate fish with onions, jalapeño, orange peel and juice, and salt to taste, for 30 minutes or more. Preheat oven to 400°. Place fish with all its marinade in a baking dish and bake uncovered 10 minutes, basting once or twice, until the fish flakes easily with a fork. The dish can be served hot or cold, garnished with orange slices.
Serves 4

Not only does this have a lot of zip, it also is a dieter's dream as it has no fat. In summer I like to prepare it in the morning and serve it cold for a light meal at night. Green Rice (p. 207) makes an excellent complement, along with a glass of dry white wine.

Seviche

1 pound thin fish fillets
1 cup lemon juice (or lime)
1 cup tomatoes, chopped (fresh or
   canned)
2 pickled jalapeños, seeded and
   minced
1/4 cup olive oil
2 tablespoons dry white wine
1 teaspoon dried basil
1/2 teaspoon dried oregano
2 tablespoons parsley, minced (or
   fresh coriander)
1 tablespoon capers
pinch of sugar
salt and freshly ground pepper
2 avocados, peeled, seeded, and
   sliced
1 red onion, cut into rings

Place fish in a glass dish and cover with the lemon juice. Leave covered in the refrigerator for several hours, turning occasionally. (This process "cooks" the fish.) Add all the other ingredients, except the avocado and onion rings. Marinate in the refrigerator for several hours and serve garnished with the avocado and onion.

Serves 4–6

Seviche is a lovely dish for hot days. It can be the main dish for lunch or supper, or make a first course for a dinner. It is particularly good for outdoor barbecues, as it keeps guests going while the meat is cooking.

Trout Frosted with Guacamole

1 tablespoon butter
1 tablespoon parsley, chopped
1 tablespoon onion, chopped
3 peppercorns
1 whole clove
1 teaspoon salt
1/2 bay leaf
1 tablespoon vinegar
1 quart water
6 whole cleaned trout
Guacamole (p. 219)
sliced ripe olives
thinly sliced radishes, cut in half

Heat butter in a large frying pan and sauté parsley and onion a few minutes until the onion softens. Add spices, bay leaf, vinegar, and water. Bring to a boil, then turn down heat and simmer 15 minutes. Poach trout in this liquid just until their flesh turns white and flakes with a fork. Remove fish carefully, then remove skin and bones, leaving the head intact. Place fish carefully back together, and chill covered in the refrigerator. To serve, coat bodies with guacamole, exposing tails and heads. Place an olive ring for an eye, and make a row of radish "scales" in the guacamole.

Serves 6

This is even prettier if you have a pastry tube and can pipe the guacamole decoratively along the fish, poking one or two rows of radish in the pipings. But no amount of decoration can improve the fine flavor. Serve it with Rice with Toasted Piñon Nuts (p. 206).

Chicken and Turkey

The Southwestern larder, as one might expect, has many exotic ways to treat chicken, as well as quite simple ones like those we all use but treated to a brilliant saucings. I've collected here some new inventions of my own devising as well as dishes old as the Aztecs and the Spanish missions. One of the delights of Southwestern kitchens, I think, is the number of ways they have of varying leftover turkey—ways of such different character that no one in the family will ever complain again that you've tried to pull Turkey Divan out of the hat once too often.

Albuquerque Baked Chicken Breasts

4 half chicken breasts
1 egg
2 tablespoons Fresh Salsa (p. 55)
1 cup bread crumbs
1 clove garlic, minced
pinch salt
1 teaspoon chili powder
1/2 teaspoon ground cumin
1/4 teaspoon dried oregano
2 tablespoons butter, melted
1 lime

Preheat oven to 375°. Remove skin from the breasts and bone them. Beat egg with salsa. Combine bread crumbs with garlic, salt, chili powder, cumin, and oregano. Whirl them in a blender or food processor to thoroughly incorporate the garlic. Dip breasts in the egg mixture, then roll in crumbs. Place in a baking dish, pour butter over, and bake 35 minutes. Serve with lime wedges.
Serves 4

This makes quite succulent chicken in a spicy crust, easy to prepare, and certainly fine enough for company.

Chicken Breasts in Pumpkinseed Sauce

4 half breasts of chicken
1 lemon
2 tablespoons butter
1 cup onion, chopped
1 clove garlic, minced
2 tablespoons sesame seeds
1/4 cup hulled pumpkin seeds
3 tablespoons chili powder
1/8 teaspoon ground cloves
1/8 teaspoon ground cinnamon
1 teaspoon dried oregano
1/2 cup tomatoes, chopped
1 cup chicken stock
salt
8 corn tortillas
oil for frying
2 tablespoons butter

Bone and skin the breasts. Flatten them to about 1/4 inch by pounding with a rolling pin between 2 pieces of waxed paper. Sprinkle with juice of half the lemon. Melt 1 tablespoon of the butter in a saucepan set over medium heat. Sauté onion and garlic until soft and place in a blender. Add the other tablespoon of butter to the pan and sauté sesame and pumpkin seeds until gold, then add them also to the blender with spices, oregano, tomatoes, and stock. Whirl smooth. Return to the saucepan and cook over low heat, stirring now and again, for 15 minutes. It will make a thick, creamy sauce which sputters. If it gets so thick it will not flow from the spoon, add a little more stock or some water. Taste for salt, and add a few drops lemon juice to perk up the sauce. Stack the tortillas and cut off the round edges to make a square, then cut the square in half and stack the halves. Cut into matchstick strips and fry in hot oil till crisp. Salt these and keep warm on paper towels. This can all be done ahead, if you wish. When ready to serve, sauté chicken breasts in 2 tablespoons butter, only 2–3 minutes a side. When springy to the touch, lift out to warm plates. Pour sauce over and sprinkle with the tortilla strips. Garnish with lemon slices if you like.

Serves 4

This is one of my favorite company dishes to show how subtle and complex this kind of cooking can be. I usually accompany it with black beans topped with sour cream and Jalapeño Salsa (p. 56), Lettuce and Radish Garnish (p. 61), and fine cold beer.

Fried Chicken with Fresh Salsa

2 tablespoons parsley, minced
1 clove garlic, minced
1/4 teaspoon dried thyme
1 teaspoon chili powder
juice of one lemon
1 teaspoon salt
1 chicken, cut up
1 egg
1/2 cup water
1/2 cup milk
1 1/2 cups flour
1/2 teaspoon salt
1 teaspoon baking soda
1 teaspoon dried thyme
1 tablespoon parsley, minced
oil for frying
Fresh Salsa (p. 55)

Chop parsley with garlic and combine with thyme, chili powder, lemon juice, and a little salt. Marinate chicken pieces in this for 2 or more hours. Drain chicken. Combine egg, water, milk, flour, salt, soda, thyme, and parsley. Dip the pieces in this batter and fry in hot oil until deep golden brown all over. The chicken is done when you can pierce it with a small knife and no blood flows after the blade. Drain on paper towels and serve with salsa.

Serves 4

When the Southwest makes fried chicken they really go all out.

Chicken with Green Chile Sauce

1 chicken, cut up
salt and freshly ground pepper
2 tablespoons butter
2 tablespoons vegetable oil
2 cups Green Chile Sauce (p. 53)

Preheat oven to 350°. Dry chicken pieces with paper towels and sprinkle with salt and pepper. Sauté them in butter and oil until golden on all sides—about 10 minutes in all. Place in a casserole, pour sauce over, and bake 20 minutes, or until hot and bubbly.

Serves 4

An excellent dish easily prepared either for a family meal or company. If you like, you can sprinkle a cup of grated Monterey Jack cheese over it for the last 5 minutes of cooking.

Chicken Casserole with Pumpkinseed Sauce

1 chicken, cut up
2 carrots, peeled and sliced
1 onion, sliced
1 tablespoon parsley
2 whole cloves
1 bay leaf
1 teaspoon dried oregano
1 teaspoon dried basil
salt and freshly ground pepper
1/2 cup hulled pumpkin seeds
1/4 cup blanched almonds
1/2 cup green chiles
1/3 cup parsley
2 cups chicken stock
1 tablespoon lemon juice
pinch of sugar
1 tablespoon butter

Put chicken in a pot with carrots, onion, parsley, cloves, herbs, and salt and pepper to taste. Add water to cover and simmer until tender, 20–25 minutes. Lift the chicken out and strip flesh from the bones. Strain the stock, skim fat off, and boil down over high heat until you have 2 cups. Preheat oven to 350°. Place pumpkin seeds, almonds, chiles, parsley, and some of the stock in a blender and whirl smooth. Place in a saucepan with the rest of the stock and cook 15 minutes, stirring until thick and smooth. Add lemon juice and a pinch of sugar, stir in butter, and cook another minute or so. Place chicken in a casserole, pour sauce over, cover, and bake 30 minutes—or until bubbly hot.
Serves 4

This delightful sauce is also good to serve with fish or even steaks, and chicken here can be replaced with leftover turkey.

Spanish Chicken Casserole

1 chicken, cut up
1/2 cup flour
1 teaspoon salt
1 teaspoon chili powder
oil for frying
4 strips bacon, minced
3 carrots, peeled and sliced
1/2 cup onion, chopped
1 4-ounce can green chiles,
    chopped
1 tablespoon parsley, minced
1 bay leaf
1/8 teaspoon dried thyme
1 lemon, sliced
2 cups tomato juice

Preheat oven to 350°. Shake chicken pieces with flour, salt, and chili powder. Fry in a little hot oil until gold—about 5 minutes a side. Place in a casserole and add all the ingredients except the lemon and tomato juice. Lay lemon slices over the top and pour tomato juice over. Bake, covered, 45 minutes.

More a family than a company dish, this is still fine fare. I serve it with Rice with Toasted Piñon Nuts (p. 206).

Mission Sesame Chicken Casserole

1 chicken
6 dried red chiles (see Ingredients; any of the chiles can be used)
4 cloves garlic, unpeeled
salt
1 tablespoon chicken fat (or butter)
1 cup onion, chopped
1 clove garlic, minced
3/4 cup canned tomatoes, drained and chopped
1/4 teaspoon dried oregano
2 tablespoons chicken fat (or butter)
3 tablespoons flour
3 cups chicken stock
1/2 cup cream
12 corn tortillas
oil for frying
salt
1/2 cup milk
grated Parmesan cheese
sesame seeds

Put chicken to boil with water to cover. Remove stems and seeds from the chiles and add them with garlic and salt to taste. Simmer over low heat an hour. Drain the stock, and reserve chicken and chiles. Refrigerate stock to let fat rise and harden (or skim fat as well as you can). Remove flesh from the chicken and discard bones. Add fat or butter to a saucepan and sauté onion and garlic until soft. Add tomatoes and oregano, mash down, and cook several minutes. Place in a blender or food processor with the reserved chiles and whirl smooth. Add 2 tablespoons fat or butter to a large saucepan and stir flour in. Cook, stirring, over low heat 6–7 minutes, or until just turning gold. Pour in 3 cups chicken stock, and let boil up as you stir. Stir in tomato mixture and cook slowly 15 minutes, tasting for salt. Add cream and chicken meat and heat through. Cut tortillas in ¹/₂-inch-by-2-inch strips and fry in hot oil until crisp. Drain on paper towels and sprinkle with salt. Preheat oven to 350°. Layer half the tortillas in a lasagna pan (or any casserole approximately 13″ × 9″). Sprinkle with half the chicken, then top with more tortillas, then the rest of the chicken. Pour milk over and sprinkle with Parmesan and sesame seeds. (This can sit covered with foil, and be cooked later if necessary.) Bake uncovered 30 minutes.

Serves 6

More than a humble casserole, this California dish is one to be as proud of as homemade lasagna—and how many dishes can we point to as serving six people bountifully from one chicken? It can be made with chili powder, if you can't get chiles, but at the cost of losing flavor, I suspect. I serve it with Refried Beans (p. 60) and bowls of sour cream, diced avocados, Lettuce and Radish Garnish (p. 61), and Parsleyed Onion Rings (p. 62) for guests to sprinkle on at will.

Emmanuel's Chicken Crepes
with Green Chile Sauce

Crepes

1/4 cup flour
1/2 teaspoon salt
2 eggs, beaten
2/3 cup milk
1 tablespoon butter, melted

Sift flour with salt, then whisk with other ingredients until smooth. Or, you may simply add all to a blender or food processor and whirl smooth, scraping down any bits of flour that cling to the sides. Pour 3–4 tablespoons at a time in a lightly greased small frying pan. Tilt the pan to spread batter out: the crepes should be about 7 inches in diameter. When they are lightly browned on one side, turn and fry for a few seconds on the other side. Set crepes aside.

Filling

1/4 cup green onions, minced with
    part of tops
2 tablespoons butter
1/2 cup tomatoes, chopped
1/2 cup almonds, ground
2/3 cup cooked chicken, diced
1 tablespoon raisins, chopped
1 tablespoon capers
10–12 green olives, chopped

Sauté onions in butter until they soften. Add tomatoes, simmer a few minutes, then add the other ingredients. Cook 5 minutes, then remove from fire. Place about a tablespoon of this mixture on each crepe, roll up, and place seam side down in a lightly buttered casserole. Preheat oven to 400°.

Sauce

2 tablespoons butter
2 tablespoons onion, grated
1 green bell pepper, grated
1½ tablespoons cornstarch
1½ cups milk
½ cup green chiles, chopped
½ cup Monterey Jack cheese,
　grated
salt

In a saucepan, sauté onion and pepper in butter over medium heat until onion softens. Dissolve cornstarch in milk and add it to the pan. Stirring all the while, simmer over low heat until mixture thickens. Add chiles, half the cheese, and salt to taste. Pour over the crepes, sprinkle with the rest of the cheese, and bake uncovered 10–12 minutes, or until the sauce begins to bubble and the crepes are lightly brown on top.
Serves 4–6

A delicious concoction from a good friend. It is a surprise here to find crepes where tortillas would usually be, to cut into such a complex filling, and have such a melting creamy sauce. Serve them with something equally delicate like Rice with Toasted Piñon Nuts (p. 206) and a tossed green salad.

Chicken (or Turkey) with Green Chiles and Sour Cream

2 cups onion, chopped
1 4-ounce can green chiles, chopped
2 tablespoons butter
2 cups cooked chicken, cut in cubes (or turkey)
1 cup sour cream
salt
1 cup Monterey Jack cheese, grated (or ¼ cup grated Parmesan)

In a saucepan, sauté onion and chiles in butter over medium heat. When soft, add chicken and cook to heat through. Add sour cream and salt to taste. This should only heat and not boil, or the sour cream will curdle. Serve with grated cheese on top, and steaming hot tortillas.

Serves 4

This makes a lovely, easy luncheon dish, but it also is one of the best fillings of all for tacos, tostadas, enchiladas, and so on.

Chicken (or Turkey) Mole

1 chicken, cut up (or ½ turkey
   breast)
1 onion, sliced
1 clove garlic
salt
1 bay leaf
2 tablespoons vegetable oil
2 tablespoons butter
Mole Sauce (pp. 57, 58)
toasted sesame seeds
lime wedges

Place chicken or turkey breast in a pot with onion, garlic, salt to taste, bay leaf, and water to cover. Simmer until just tender and remove from the pot. The chicken can remain as is, but turkey should be skinned and cut into 1-inch cubes. Preheat oven to 350°. Sauté chicken or turkey in oil and butter until the meat begins to brown lightly, then place in a casserole. Pour sauce over and bake uncovered 30 minutes. Serve sprinkled with sesame seeds which have been placed in a dry frying pan and shaken over low heat until golden. Garnish with lime wedges.

Chicken serves 4; turkey serves 6–8

A Mole is one of the wonders of this cuisine, and it is usually served only at holidays, when whole turkeys are transformed with this rich and subtle sauce. I don't wait, and serve it all the time to guests with either a chicken or one of the turkey pieces that are easily available now all year round—the breast being the choicest if you don't cook it so much it dries out. A mole gains in flavor by being reheated the second day.

Turkey with Garbanzo Stuffing

Stuff your turkey with Garbanzo Purée (p. 204), then roast in your favorite manner. At serving time remove the stuffing and place in a serving dish. Pour some of the juices from the pan over the top and sprinkle with toasted and salted piñon nuts.

Serves 8–12

Garbanzos aren't quite as good as chestnuts, but in this they come near it.

Additional Recipes Which May Use Turkey

Calabacitas Soup (p. 37)
Texas Turkey Enchilada Casserole (p. 76)
Chicken Mole Enchiladas (p. 80)
Chicken (or Turkey) and Green Chile Pie (p. 82)
Chicken Tacos with Green Chile Sauce (p. 96)
Chicken Casserole with Pumpkinseed Sauce (p. 130)
Chicken Filling for Tamale Pie (p. 172)

Meats

Many of the foods most typical of the Southwest are sparing of meat, though much care and tradition are put into spicing and saucing what meat there is. But Texans particularly are proud of their succulent seared steaks, and recipes are to be found from all over for chops and joints and other cuts of meat, suitable for serving with a vegetable and a crisp salad, rather than the beans and shredded lettuce we expect on a combination platter.

Baked Pork Loin with Oranges

3-pound boned pork loin roast
salt and freshly ground pepper
2 pickled jalapeños, seeded and
  minced
3 slices bacon
1/2 cup onion, minced
1 clove garlic, minced
1 banana, mashed
1 cup orange juice
1 tablespoon chili powder
orange slices

Preheat oven to 350°. Place most of fat from the pork in a frying pan over medium high heat. When it releases a couple of tablespoons of liquid fat, remove the pieces of fat and brown roast on all sides. Take from the frying pan and place in a roaster. Salt and pepper it well, sprinkle with jalapeños, then lay bacon slices over. Combine onion, garlic, banana, orange juice, and chili powder (a food processor is useful for making this sauce) and pour over the meat. Bake, covered, for 1 1/2 hours. Baste meat with the sauce several times as it cooks. Remove roast for carving. Skim most of the fat from the sauce and stir it over high heat until smooth. Slice meat and serve with sauce over it. Garnish with orange slices.
Serves 6

An unusual dish, and one of my favorites from the whole repertoire. The combination of onion, garlic, banana, orange juice, and chiles may seem strange—but wait till you smell their delicious cooking odors!

Carnitas

1 pork shoulder roast (4–5 pounds)
salt
$^1/_2$ teaspoon cumin seeds
$^1/_2$ teaspoon coriander seeds
$^1/_2$ teaspoon dried oregano
2 onions, chopped
1 clove garlic, peeled
2 carrots, peeled and sliced

Put pork in a kettle with water to cover, some salt, and all the other ingredients. Bring to a boil, lower heat, and simmer 2$^1/_2$ hours. Heat oven to 350°. Remove the roast to a baking pan and bake uncovered 45 minutes to an hour—or until meat is browned. Remove from oven, cut out as much fat as possible, and shred the meat.

Serves 6–8

Most recipes for carnitas are simply cubes of pork salted, peppered, and roasted for cocktail nibbles. But this recipe from a San Francisco taquería is something else again. All that boiling and baking produces a meat both soft and crispy at the edges, and it makes one of the finest fillings for burritos or tacos I know (with beans and salsa). It also makes a fine basis for a tamale pie. It's best to prepare it for a fairly large party, though, as the pork is not nearly so good after it has been refrigerated.

Tinga

2 cups cooked pork (or Carnitas
  [p. 144])
1 tablespoon bacon fat (or oil)
$^{1}/_{2}$ cup onion, chopped
1 clove garlic, minced
$^{1}/_{2}$ cup Chorizo (p. 146)
1 cup tomatoes, chopped
salt
1 pickled jalapeño, seeded and
  minced
$^{1}/_{2}$ cup stock (preferably from the
  Carnitas)
Parsleyed Onion Rings (p. 62)
sliced avocados

Trim meat of any fat and shred it. Melt bacon fat or oil in a frying pan and sauté onion and garlic over medium heat until soft. Add chorizo and cook 10 more minutes, stirring to crumble it. Add tomatoes, salt to taste, the jalapeño, shredded pork, and stock. Cook over high heat until all the liquid is cooked away and the meat begins to brown slightly. Serve with onion rings and avocados.

Serves 4

This can be served as is, with beans and shredded lettuce, but I like it best as a filling for tacos or tostadas.

Chorizo

1 pound lean ground pork
1 teaspoon salt
1¹/₂–2 tablespoons powdered red
    chile
¹/₄ teaspoon each ground cloves,
    cinnamon, dried oregano,
    thyme, cumin, and black pepper
pinch each of ginger, nutmeg, and
    ground coriander
1 crumbled bay leaf
4 cloves garlic, minced
1 tablespoon vinegar

If you have the pork ground at the market have them grind it twice since it should not be too coarse. Or you can take it and whirl it a few times in a food processor if need be. Mix with other ingredients and let it stand covered in the refrigerator 24 hours to mellow. It will keep another day or so, but after that it should be frozen in small batches or in patties. Most of the recipes in this book call for chorizo as a crumbled ingredient, but it can be cooked in patties as you would any bulk sausage.

Chorizo, except in some places in the Southwest, is a very chancey buy at the store—some of it passable and most downright awful. It's so easy to make and freeze in batches, though, I see no reason to bother with store-bought.

Pork Chops with Kidney Beans

6 pork chops ¹/₂–³/₄ inch thick
salt and freshly ground pepper
¹/₄ cup olive oil (or vegetable oil)
2 cups water
2 cups onions, chopped
2 cloves garlic, minced
2 tablespoons olive oil (or
  vegetable oil)
¹/₂ cup fresh green chiles, cut into
  strips
4 drops Tabasco sauce
3 cups cooked kidney beans (or
  canned)
¹/₂ cup Cheddar cheese, grated
Parsleyed Onion Rings (p. 62)

Trim chops of fat and sprinkle with salt and pepper. Place a little oil in a frying pan and brown the chops over high heat. Add water, cover, and cook over low heat 30 minutes. In another pan sauté onions and garlic in the rest of the oil until onion softens. Add chiles, Tabasco, and beans. Pour this over the chops, cover, and cook over low heat another 30 minutes. Serve with cheese sprinkled over and the onion rings.

Serves 6

A splendid hearty family dish served with hot tortillas, a salad, and frosty beer.

Garbanzo and Chorizo Casserole

1 pound dried garbanzos
salt
3 slices of bacon, diced
1/2 cup green onion, chopped with
    part of tops
1 green bell pepper, chopped
2 cloves garlic, minced
1 cup Chorizo (p. 146)
1 cup tomato sauce
1/4 teaspoon ground cumin
3/4 tablespoon chili powder
3/4 cup pitted ripe olives
1/4 cup fresh coriander (or parsley)

Soak garbanzos overnight in plenty of water, then drain and cover with fresh water. Bring to a boil in a large pot, lower heat, and simmer until very tender—4–5 hours. Add salt to taste the last hour of cooking. Preheat oven to 375°. Place bacon in a frying pan and cook until done but not crisp. Remove from the pan and sauté onion, pepper, and garlic in the bacon fat. When onion is tender, add the mixture to the bacon. Make chorizo into walnut-size balls and sauté them over high heat in the frying pan. When brown, remove from pan and pour any fat off. Add tomato sauce, cumin, chili powder, and the onion mixture. Simmer 5 minutes, then add olives and coriander. Mix this sauce with drained garbanzos, $1/2$ cup of the liquid the garbanzos were cooked in, and place in a casserole. Top with chorizo balls, cover, and bake 30–45 minutes, or until hot and bubbly.

Serves 6

A delightful Spanish-influenced dish fine for a hearty family dinner. It can be speeded up by using a couple of large cans of garbanzos, if you wish.

Tucson Cassoulet

2 cups black beans (or kidney or pinto)
1/2 pound pork loin (about 2 thick chops)
1/2 pound Chorizo (p. 146)
1 large onion, chopped
2 cloves garlic, minced
2/3 cup green chiles, chopped
salt
4 corn tortillas, cut in matchstick strips
oil for frying
1 1/2 cups Monterey Jack cheese, grated
1/4 cup fresh coriander, minced (optional)

Soak beans in water overnight (or use the quick soak method). Discard water, and add enough more water to come about 2 inches over the beans. Cook for an hour, or until almost tender. Cut pork into small dice and add to the bean pot (along with bones if you use chops). Roll chorizo into large marbles and add them, along with onion, garlic, and chiles. Add salt to taste. Simmer 2 more hours, making sure there is always a little liquid in the pot. If it gets dry, add hot—not cold—water. Preheat oven to 325°. Remove any bones from the pot, and drain beans in a colander, saving the juices. Place in a shallow casserole large enough to hold about a 2-inch layer of beans, and add enough bean liquid to moisten well. Fry tortillas in hot oil until crisp, and drain on paper towels. Sprinkle lightly with salt. Scatter them over the beans. Bake 30 minutes, and at the very end sprinkle cheese and coriander over and let it melt.

Serves 4–6

A rich, delightful casserole that needs only a tossed salad to make an admirable meal.

Chorizo Chilaquiles

8 corn tortillas
oil for frying
3/4 cup Chorizo (p. 146)
1/2 cup onion, chopped
1 clove garlic, minced
1/2 cup tomato sauce
1 pickled jalapeño, seeded and
   minced
1/4 teaspoon ground red chile
pinch of sugar
1/2 cup ripe olives (optional)
1 1/2 cups Monterey Jack cheese,
   grated
1/4 cup Parmesan cheese
1 avocado, peeled, seeded and
   sliced
Parsleyed Onion Rings (p. 62)

Preheat oven to 350°. Cut tortillas into small strips and fry in hot oil just until softened. Remove with a slotted spoon and drain on paper towels. Discard oil, place pan back on the fire, and fry chorizo until it begins to crisp. Remove from the pan and add onion and garlic. Cook until soft, then add the tomato sauce, jalapeño, ground chile, and sugar. Cook another 5 minutes, then remove from heat. Place a layer of tortillas in the bottom of a casserole, then some chorizo, then tomato sauce, then olives, then the cheeses. Repeat layers and place in the oven. Bake 20 minutes, or until hot and bubbly. Serve with avocado slices and onion rings on top.

Serves 4

Chilaquiles come in many versions—it is a name usually given to any dish that layers tortillas, sauce, meats, and what not. This one with chorizo is a particularly fine example, I think, and it makes almost a meal in itself.

Picadillo

¹/₂ pound ground beef
¹/₂ pound ground pork
1 cup onion, chopped
2 cloves garlic, minced
1 cup canned tomatoes, chopped
1 tablespoon vinegar
pinch of sugar
¹/₂ teaspoon ground cinnamon
pinch of ground cloves
¹/₄ teaspoon ground cumin
1 teaspoon salt
1 bay leaf
3 drops Tabasco sauce
¹/₂ cup seedless raisins
¹/₂ cup green olives, chopped
   (optional)
¹/₂ cup blanched, slivered almonds

Stir meats in a frying pan over high heat. When they begin to release fat, add onion and garlic. As the meat starts to brown, pour off fat and add all other ingredients except raisins, olives, and almonds. Simmer, covered, 30 minutes. Add water or stock if necessary, but not too much, for when done the picadillo should be moist but not soupy. Finally, add raisins, olives, and almonds and cook 10 more minutes.

Serves 4

Picadillo is wonderful served over plain boiled rice, but in the Southwest it is more often a stuffing for tacos, tamales, chicken, or best of all—green chiles.

Carne Adovada

3 pounds boned pork loin, or beef
  flank steak
2 cups thick Red Chile Sauce
  (p. 51)
$1/4$ teaspoon ground coriander
$1/8$ teaspoon ground cumin
2 tablespoons vinegar

Cut meat in bite-size cubes or strips. Place in a bowl and stir in chile sauce, spices, and vinegar. Cover, and marinate in the refrigerator 24 hours. To cook, spread out meat and marinade in a baking dish or roasting pan, add $1/4$ inch water, cover the pan with foil, and bake at 325° for $1^{1/2}$ hours. If the meat gets dry, add a little more water. For beef you will need a little oil dribbled over, so check after the first hour to see how it's going.

Serves 6

Fiery carne adovada freezes well, so I always make a large batch and put some away for other meals. I like to serve it with plain rice with cubes of avocado tossed in at the last minute with the butter, and of course it makes a splendid filling for tacos, burritos or tostadas.

Carne Adovada with Jicama

4 cups Carne Adovada (p. 154)
2 cups jicama, peeled and cut in
   $1/2$-inch dice
2 tablespoons butter
salt
1 clove garlic, minced
1 teaspoon lime juice
2 tablespoons fresh coriander (or
   parsley)
$1/4$ cup piñon nuts
1 tablespoon vegetable oil
lime wedges

Warm meat in a saucepan. Pat jicama dry with paper towels. Heat butter in a frying pan over high heat, and when it sizzles add jicama and fry 5 minutes, tossing now and again, until it starts to brown on all sides. Sprinkle with a little salt, add garlic, and toss another minute. Add lime juice, cover, turn heat down low, and cook 10–12 minutes, or until done through but still crisp. Toss with coriander and remove from heat. Sauté piñon nuts in a little oil until they are slightly golden. To serve, place carne adovada on a plate, top with some of the jicama, and sprinkle with nuts. Garnish with lime wedges.

Serves 4

A wonderful (if untraditional) dish. The crispy jicama takes a little of the heat off the Carne Adovada, and provides contrast in texture at the same time. I serve it with Green Rice (p. 207).

Santa Fe Steak

3 pounds round steak
salt
$^1/_2$ teaspoon powdered red chile
1 clove garlic, minced
4 tablespoons flour
3 tablespoons vegetable oil
3 cups onion, chopped
1 green bell pepper, chopped
1 tablespoon chili powder
1 cup tomatoes, chopped
$^1/_2$ cup beef stock

Trim steak of fat and cut into serving portions. Rub with a little salt, the chile, garlic, and flour. Pound with a meat tenderizer. Heat oil in a large frying pan and brown pieces on both sides over high heat. Remove meat, turn down heat, and sauté onions and pepper in the pan until soft. Add meat, with chili powder, tomatoes, and stock. Cover the pan and simmer $1^1/_2$–2 hours, or until meat is very tender. (Check now and again, and if it dries out add some more stock or water.)
Serves 4–6

This is "Swiss" steak in the Southwestern manner. And I like to serve it like Swiss steak, with fluffy mashed potatoes to catch the sauce. For a nice touch, try folding minced fresh coriander into the potatoes.

Stuffed Chile Meatloaf

1½ pounds lean ground beef
1⅓ cup Chile Meat Sauce (p. 54)
salt
1 cup cooked pinto beans
⅓ cup green chiles, chopped
¾ cup Cheddar cheese, grated

Preheat oven to 350°. Mix meat with 1 cup of the sauce and salt to taste—not too much, since the sauce is well seasoned. Line bottom and sides of a loaf pan with ¾ of the meat. Mash beans and add green chile and cheese. Fill the pocket made in the pan with this, then carefully top beans with the rest of the meat so that the loaf is completely covered and sealed in. Spread the last of the sauce over the top and bake 1 hour.
Serves 4–6

I think this makes one of the finest meatloaves going. It is, certainly, a family dish, but one that gets called for again and again.

New Mexican Meatloaf

1 pound lean ground beef
1/2 cup Chorizo (p. 146)
1/2 cup ripe olives, chopped
1/2 cup onion, chopped
1/2 cup cornmeal
1/2 cup green chiles, chopped
1 pickled jalapeño, seeded and
   minced
1 teaspoon chili powder
1/2 teaspoon dried oregano
pinch of ground cumin
salt to taste
avocado slices

Preheat oven to 350°. Combine all ingredients except the avocado. Pack lightly into a greased loaf pan. Bake for an hour. Serve with slices of avocado on top of the loaf—and Fresh Salsa if you wish.
   Serves 4–6

This spicy loaf is usually served with pinto beans and the regular garnishes, but it is also fine with plain mashed potatoes and some such vegetable as Calabacitas (p. 189).

Cumin Liver

1¹/₂ pounds beef liver, sliced
1 lemon, grated rind and juice
¹/₄ teaspoon ground cumin
¹/₈ teaspoon chili powder
pinch of ground allspice
freshly ground pepper
¹/₂ teaspoon dried oregano
¹/₂ cup vegetable oil
2 tablespoons butter
2 tablespoons vegetable oil
salt
1 lemon, quartered
1 avocado, peeled, seeded and
   sliced

Trim liver, cutting off the membrane on the outer edges, and cutting out any tough tubes or what have you. Make a marinade of lemon rind and juice, the spices and oregano, and oil. Marinate liver slices for an hour or so. Drain and pat dry with paper towels. Heat butter and oil in a frying pan and sauté liver over high heat only about 3 minutes a side. The outside ought to be seared and golden, but the insides still pink (to my taste). Salt lightly, and arrange on plates with lemon and avocado slices.

Serves 4

The marinade here makes inexpensive beef liver into something all but the most dedicated liver-haters will enjoy. Serve it with a vegetable such as Calabacitas (p. 189) or San Antonio Cream Peas (p. 194).

Stew with Squash

1½ pounds stew meat (beef or lamb)
1 cup green beans, cut up
6 ears corn, cut in 1-inch pieces
6 squash blossoms (or zucchini), cut in ½-inch slices
¼ cup green onions, chopped with part of tops
1 clove garlic, minced
2 tablespoons fresh coriander (or parsley)
salt and freshly ground pepper
pinch of sugar
3 drops Tabasco sauce

Stew meat in a pot with water to cover until just tender—the time will depend on type of meat and size of cubes. Add all the other ingredients and simmer 30 more minutes.

Serves 4

Most stews in the Southwest are heavily laced with either red or green chile, and while these are very tasty I like this simple one with all the flavor of a summer garden.

Lamb Ribs with Red Chile Sauce

2 whole lamb breasts
salt
1½ cups Red Chile Sauce (p. 51)

Trim the fell and fat from the lamb. There is a good layer of fat on the top which should be trimmed down as far as the first layer of meat, as well as other bits and pieces of fat. Cut the breasts in 2-rib portions, rub with salt and place in a large bowl. Pour sauce over, and toss to coat completely. Let marinate in the refrigerator 6 hours or so. Preheat oven to 400°. Lay the ribs bone side up in a pan large enough to hold them all in one layer. Bake 30 minutes, turn over, and bake another 30 minutes.

Serves 4

Lamb breast is a little-used meat, for some reason. I like these ribs very much—they are a little fatty, but they have all the lamb flavor you could ask at very little cost.

Leg of Lamb in Chile and Wine Sauce

leg of lamb, boned
1 cup red wine
1/2 cup orange juice
1 tablespoon chili powder
1/4 cup green chiles, chopped
2 tablespoons olive oil (or
    vegetable oil)
1 medium onion, chopped
2 cloves garlic, minced
1/2 teaspoon dried oregano
1 teaspoon ground cumin
1 tablespoon brown sugar
1 bay leaf
grated rind of one orange
1 teaspoon salt

Have lamb boned at market. This is not absolutely necessary, but it makes for better marinating and cutting. Remove most of fat and the fell which covers the meat and place lamb in a large bowl. Combine all ingredients and marinate in refrigerator for 24 hours. Turn several times during this period. Preheat oven to 450°. Lift meat out, drain, and place on a rack in a roaster. Cook 15 minutes, then turn heat down to 350° and pour marinade around the meat. Cook 25 minutes a pound for pink lamb, 30 minutes for well done. If lamb has not been boned, subtract 5 minutes per pound. When ready to serve, remove meat to platter and let sit at room temperature 10–15 minutes. Skim off fat from the pan juices and serve in a sauce boat with the meat.

Serves 8

A splendidly spicy roast that I like to serve with Saffron Rice with Stuffed Green Chiles (p. 205). If you have an outdoor grill you can have the butcher butterfly the lamb when he bones it. After marinating it can be grilled 25–30 minutes per side.

Desert Rabbit

1 2½–3-pound rabbit, cut up
2 cloves garlic, peeled and slightly
   flattened
½ cup vegetable oil
2 tablespoons red wine vinegar
¼ teaspoon dried oregano
freshly ground pepper
2 tablespoons vegetable oil
1 large onion, chopped
¾ cup tomato, chopped
¼ cup green chile, chopped
1 tablespoon chili powder
¼ teaspoon ground cumin
1 tablespoon fresh coriander,
   chopped (optional)
⅛ teaspoon ground coriander
salt
1 cup beer
½ cup sour cream

The day before, put rabbit in a bowl with garlic, oil, vinegar, oregano, and plenty of ground pepper. Stir, cover, and marinate overnight in the refrigerator. The next day wipe rabbit dry with paper towels. Heat oil in a large frying pan and sauté rabbit over medium high heat until golden on both sides. Stir in onion and cook until soft. Add tomato, green chile, spices and herbs, salt to taste, and beer. Cover, turn heat down low, and simmer 40 minutes—or until rabbit is done. Remove the rabbit pieces to warm plates, stir sour cream into the pan juices (if mixture looks very soupy, reduce over high heat a few minutes). Spoon sauce over the rabbit pieces, and serve.
Serves 4

A full-flavored but still mild recipe for rabbit fanciers (among whom I count myself). It should be served with something like Texas Spoonbread (p. 209) or perhaps creamy mashed potatoes mixed with minced fresh coriander, to use all that beautiful sauce on.

Tamale Pies

I once helped make tamales—a process that took two days, three people, and several ingredients completely unavailable outside the Southwest. No wonder they are usually made for Christmas feasts only! I've never wanted to try again, for though they were very good they didn't seem worth all that time and effort. So rather than write pages and pages of the real right way to turn out a tamale, I'll simply give some quick and easy variations on the Tamale Pie—itself a goodly dish.

Tamale Mixture I

2 cups masa harina
1¹/₃ cups hot water
1 cup cream
¹/₄ cup butter
4 eggs, separated
1 teaspoon salt
1 teaspoon baking powder
¹/₄ cup Parmesan cheese

Blend masa with hot water, then with cream. Melt butter and add to the mixture, beating in thoroughly. Add egg yolks, one by one, still beating, then stir in salt and baking powder. Beat egg whites stiff, but not dry, and fold in lightly. Place half in the bottom of a 2-quart casserole, add a filling, then top with the rest of the tamale mixture. Bake 45 minutes at 350°, then sprinkle with cheese and cook 15 more minutes.

A rich fluffy topping, fine with any type of filling.

Tamale Mixture II

1¹/₂ cups milk
1 teaspoon salt
2 tablespoons butter
¹/₂ cup cornmeal
1 cup Monterey Jack cheese,
    grated
2 eggs, beaten

Heat milk almost to boiling, then add salt and butter. Stir cornmeal into the milk slowly, beating constantly to prevent lumps—a wire whisk is good for this. Simmer 15 minutes, making sure the mixture doesn't burn on the bottom. Remove from fire and mix in cheese and eggs. Line both sides and bottom of a 1¹/₂-quart soufflé dish, pour in a filling, and cover with the rest of the mash. Bake at 350° for 1 hour.

This makes a slightly denser mixture than Filling I, but nice and tasty from the cheese.

Tamale Mixture III

2 cups blue cornmeal (or masa
    harina)
2 teaspoons salt
6 cups boiling water (or beef or
    chicken stock)

Stir cornmeal slowly into boiling salted water. (If you use stock it probably won't need any salt.) Stir until smooth and thickened, then cook over very low heat 15 minutes, stirring as it cooks to make sure the bottom doesn't burn. Line a 2-quart casserole with the mush, pour a filling in, and cover with the rest of the mush. Bake at 350° for an hour.

If you are able to obtain New Mexico's fine blue cornmeal, then be sure to try this recipe. It is the simplest kind of tamale mixture, but the extra flavor of blue cornmeal makes it a very special one.

Chicken Cheese Tamale Pie

Filling

1 chicken
3 large onions
2 cloves garlic
1 bay leaf
1 teaspoon dried basil
2 whole cloves
3 peppercorns
$1/2$ teaspoon salt
$1/3$ cup green chiles, chopped
1 pickled jalapeño, seeded and
　minced
1 cup ripe olives, chopped
salt
pinch of sugar
1 teaspoon chili powder
2 cups sour cream
2 cups Monterey Jack cheese,
　grated

Put chicken in a pot with onions, garlic, herbs, spices, and salt. Simmer 30 minutes, or until tender. Remove chicken, and strip flesh from the bones. Strain stock and reserve 2 cups for the tamale mixture. Chop chicken and the onions it was cooked with, and combine with chiles, jalapeño, olives, salt to taste, sugar, chili powder, and sour cream. Place in the bottom of a casserole. Top with grated cheese. Preheat oven to 375°.

Tamale Mixture

2 cups chicken stock
1 cup masa harina
2 eggs, separated
$1/2$ cup Monterey Jack cheese,
    grated
whole ripe olives

Put stock in a saucepan and bring it to a boil. Add masa gradually, beating constantly. Cook over very low heat 5–10 minutes, stirring until thickened. Remove from fire and stir in egg yolks. Whip whites stiff, but not dry, and fold into the mush. Spread over the filling in the casserole, sprinkle with cheese, and decorate with olives. Bake at 375° 30–40 minutes, or until bubbly and golden on top.
Serves 6

A most sumptuous tamale pie, with subtle flavors and texture, and fit for any company.

Chicken Filling

2 tablespoons butter
1/2 cup onion, finely chopped
2 cups tomatoes, chopped
1/2 cup green chiles, chopped
2 cups cooked chicken, diced
12 stuffed green olives, chopped
1/2 cup raisins
1/4 cup ground almonds
salt to taste

Melt butter in a saucepan and sauté onion until it is soft. Add tomatoes and cook a few minutes more. Add the rest of the ingredients—be sure to taste for salt as the olives are already salty. Simmer 5–10 minutes.

The addition of olives, raisins, and almonds gives this filling a special lift.

Beef Filling

¹/₄ cup olive oil (or vegetable oil)
1 cup onion, chopped
¹/₂ cup green bell pepper, chopped
1 clove garlic, minced
1¹/₂ pounds ground beef
2¹/₂ cups canned tomatoes (with juice)
salt and freshly ground pepper
2 tablespoons chili powder
¹/₂ cup cornmeal
1 cup water
1 cup ripe olives, chopped

In a frying pan, sauté onion, pepper, and garlic in oil until softened. Scrape into a bowl and reserve. Add beef to the pan and cook over high heat, stirring to crumble as it cooks. When it begins to brown, scrape it out onto absorbent paper to remove as much grease as possible. Return to the pan with onion mixture, add tomatoes, salt and pepper to taste, and chili powder. Simmer 10 minutes. Stir cornmeal into water and add it to the meat. Cook over low heat another 10 minutes—or until smooth and thickened. Finally, add olives.

The most common kind of tamale filling, and it can be adjusted to any taste. Some people add much more chili powder, perhaps with some jalapeño or other such hotness, and chopped fresh coriander can give it an added zing too.

Pork Filling

2 pounds pork
¹/₂ cup water
2 cloves garlic
salt and freshly ground pepper
¹/₂ cup onion, chopped
1 cup tomatoes, chopped
1 4-ounce can green chiles,
  chopped
3 tablespoons fresh coriander,
  minced (optional)
¹/₈ teaspoon ground coriander

Cut fat off pork and cut meat into cubes. Place in a frying pan with water, garlic, and salt and pepper to taste. Cook over high heat until water is absorbed and meat begins to brown in its own fat. Add onion and cook several minutes over medium heat to soften. Add tomatoes, chiles, and both corianders. Cover, and cook over low heat 30 minutes.

A very tasty filling, good in itself as a main dish with the addition of a cup of corn or hominy. If you have fresh coriander, this is a fine way to see how it acts with ground coriander—though they taste different, together they seem to have a synergistic effect that perfumes the whole dish.

Barbecues

All Americans dote on their outdoor grills, particularly in hot weather, but it is perhaps in the Southwestern states that the barbecue is brought closest to a fine art. Everyone has his own secret sauce, or can argue the benefits of mesquite or hickory. A lot of time and care may be needed before a guest arrives, but in no time at all the host usually presents a wide range of foods from the grill—corn in the husk, fillings for tacos, slabs of juicy meat, tender vegetables. Of course the famous Texas barbecue parties, where whole beeves are basted overnight, are the best known, but they are done by professionals and are quite outside the means of a home cook.

Carne Asada

2 pounds skirt steak
salt and freshly ground pepper
Fresh Salsa (p. 55)

Trim the steak of all membrane and fat (this is usually done by the butcher before you buy skirt steak, but inspect the meat to make sure). If the steak is in one long piece cut it up to make strips easily grilled. Grill over hot charcoal for several minutes a side, or to taste: the meat should be well browned on the outside and still pink within. Salt and pepper as the meat cooks. Remove to a chopping board and either cut across the grain into serving portions or chop into bite-size pieces for stuffing tacos or burritos. Either way serve with fresh salsa.
Serves 4

Skirt steaks are exceptionally tender and—if you can find them—still inexpensive. They make one of the best fillings I know of for a taco or burrito, needing little else but some pinto beans, a salsa, and perhaps cheese. They can be panfried, but there is no substitute for the smoky grilled taste they acquire cooked outside over a hickory or mesquite fire.

Grilled Steaks

After experimenting with marinades and whatnot, I find that they really do tenderize inferior cuts, but that it's best to go ahead and buy a fine steak at least 1½ inches thick and put nothing on it at all. If you do want to grill a steak that doesn't seem to have much fat marbled through it, make a simple marinade of wine, oil, ground pepper, and a garlic clove (no salt—save that for the very end). Anything that good doesn't need a sauce, but you might like to serve a bowl of Jalapeño Salsa (p. 56) on the side, or have a bowl of Guacamole (p. 219) to slather on the hot steaks. Guacamole is always thought of as a salad, but it makes a superior and unexpected sauce for any hot meat.

Bill Benton's Chili Burgers

Mix lean ground beef with a little finely grated onion, a bit of cream to moisten, and quite a bit of freshly ground pepper. Don't salt the meat until it is cooked! Serve with warm buns, hot Chile Meat Sauce (p. 54) to slather over them, and bowls of chopped mild onion, grated cheese, Lettuce and Radish Garnish (p. 61), and Fresh Salsa (p. 55) for diners to add as they wish. These burgers, of course, may either be grilled outside or panfried until they are brown on the outside and still a bit pink in the middle.

When you make Chile Meat Sauce keep these glorious sloppy burgers in mind, and make enough to have some on hand in the freezer. Everyone in the family will bless you for it.

John Bigelow's Hamburgers with Guacamole

Combine ground beef with chopped green chiles and shape into patties. Grill or panfry until crusty brown on the outside and pink on the inside, and serve on warm buns spread with Guacamole (p. 219). Salt lightly before serving.

In the Southwest they don't necessarily insist that hamburgers should have a slice of tomato, a leaf of lettuce, and a melt of cheese. They use what is at hand, and make wonderful burgers—once you've tried them with Guacamole you may want never to go back to the tomato and lettuce.

Grilled Lamb Patties

1 pound ground lamb
6 tablespoons piñon nuts
1 tablespoon vegetable oil
1 teaspoon chili powder
1/4 teaspoon ground coriander
1/8 teaspoon ground cumin
salt
1/3 cup ice water

Put meat in a bowl. Sauté nuts in oil until they are lightly golden all over, then drain on paper towels. Mix nuts, spices, and salt to taste lightly into the meat. Add ice water bit by bit until it is all incorporated. Shape into four patties and refrigerate 2 hours before grilling. They should cook about 5 minutes per side whether over charcoal or panfried.
Serves 4

Not all butchers grind up their lesser cuts of lamb for sale, but when you find one who does, make sure you snap some up. It is inexpensive but still has all the wonderful flavor of lamb.

Barbecue Spareribs

5 pounds pork spareribs
salt and freshly ground pepper
paprika
2 cloves garlic, minced
1/2 cup white wine
juice of 1 lemon
pinch of sugar
barbecue sauce

Cut ribs into serving pieces and rub with salt, pepper, and some paprika. Place in a bowl and add garlic, wine, lemon juice, and a little sugar. Toss well and marinate in the refrigerator several hours or overnight. Grill over a charcoal fire brushing with your favorite barbecue sauce every 10 minutes or so. (Whatever sauce you use, try adding a tablespoon of chili powder, and maybe even a minced pickled jalapeño for hotness.) The ribs should be cooked 4 inches above the coals, and they will take 1 hours and 15 minutes to cook. Or they may be baked in a 350° oven for about 1 1/2 hours.

Serves 6

The way I look at it, spareribs are good practically any way they are cooked, but these are particularly pleasing.

Spicy Pork Chops

3 tablespoons chili powder
3 tablespoons tomato juice
4 cloves garlic, minced
salt
¼ teaspoon dried oregano
8 pork chops

Combine chili powder, tomato juice, garlic, salt to taste, and oregano. Spread this on both sides of the chops and marinate several hours or overnight. These can either be grilled about 4 inches above a charcoal fire for 15–20 minutes a side, or browned in a frying pan, then cooked with a little water in a 350° oven for 45 minutes. Serve with Fresh Salsa (p. 55).
Serves 4

The trick to these is cooking them slowly so they cook through but do not dry out. If they start to look dry, brush some oil on them as they cook.

Veal (or Lamb) Chops

8 chops about 1¹/2 inches thick
¹/2 teaspoon each dried thyme,
    ground cumin, and dried
    oregano
1 tablespoon chili powder
salt
1 cup onion, chopped
¹/3 cup red wine
¹/4 cup olive oil
¹/2 cup tomato sauce
1 clove garlic, minced
1 teaspoon lime juice (or lemon)

If the chops are lamb, they need to be trimmed of as much fat as possible. Veal chops don't need to be trimmed. Combine all ingredients and marinate chops at least 4 hours. Cook over a charcoal fire basting with some of the marinade. Lamb will take only 5–7 minutes a side to brown on the outside but remain pink in the middle, but veal should cook slowly higher over the coals.

Serves 4

The best chops for this are the veal—particularly ones with the kidney still left in them. Lamb chops don't really need any marinade to be grilled, but this does give them a nice piquant quality.

Barbecue Shrimp

1 pound shrimp
$^1/_2$ cup butter, melted
1 tablespoon lemon juice
$1^1/_2$ teaspoons chili powder
salt and freshly ground pepper
$^1/_8$ teaspoon dried oregano

The shrimp for these can be either shelled or not. Some people like to crack the savory shells as they eat—rather messy, but good—and some don't want the bother. I like them either way. Combine the butter, lemon juice, chili powder, salt and pepper to taste, and the oregano, and brush shrimp as they cook. They will need only a few minutes a side until they turn pink and start to brown.

Serves 2 as a main dish, 4 for appetizers

Most people can eat these like popcorn—the more the better.

185

Barbecue Chicken

1 chicken, whole or cut up
1 cup white wine
$^1/_2$ cup orange juice
1 tablespoon chili powder
$^1/_4$ cup green chiles, chopped
2 tablespoons olive oil
1 small onion, chopped
2 cloves garlic, minced
$^1/_2$ teaspoon dried oregano
1 teaspoon ground cumin
1 tablespoon brown sugar
1 bay leaf
grated rind of one orange
salt

Combine everything and marinate several hours or overnight. A whole chicken can be spit-roasted, or the pieces can be grilled, basting every 5 minutes with the marinade. The chicken is done when a small knife poked in the leg or thigh does not draw any blood.

Serves 4

Of course you can bake either a whole chicken or the parts in a 350° oven for 40–45 minutes, but nothing can take the place of hickory or mesquite smoke perfuming the bird.

Vegetables and Starches

The irrigated gardens of these dry states grow a bounty, and everybody eats broccoli just as you and I do, with plain butter and lemon juice. They also liven their vegetables with chiles and fresh coriander—particularly delightful with corn and summer squash. Things like Calabacitas and Green Corn Cakes are wonderful all year long, and with many another kind of cooking. Unusual vegetables such as tender cactus, jicama, squash flowers, and wild lamb's quarters come into their own here. And there is also that glorification of the green chile, Chiles Rellenos, fit for commoner or king, as well as fluffy rice tossed with piñon nuts, which gourmets everywhere should savor.

Calabacitas

3 tablespoons butter
1 small onion, chopped
1 clove garlic, peeled and slightly
    flattened
1 pound summer squash, sliced (or
    zucchini)
1/4 cup green chile, chopped
1 cup fresh corn (2–3 ears)
1/2 cup tomato, chopped (optional)
1/4 teaspoon dried mint (optional)
salt and freshly ground pepper

Melt butter in a frying pan and sauté onion and garlic over medium heat until softened. Remove the garlic and add squash, chile, corn, and tomato if you use it. Stir well and add mint and salt and pepper to taste. Cover, lower heat, and cook about 5 minutes, or until the vegetables are done, but still a bit crisp.

Serves 4–6

This Southwestern succotash has many variations, but any way you put it together is a delight, particularly with fresh garden vegetables. You can use half yellow summer squash and half zucchini, and sometimes diced cream cheese is stirred in just before serving.

Squash Flower Pancakes

2 cups summer squash (or
    zucchini), grated
$^1/_2$ cup flour
1 teaspoon baking powder
$^1/_2$ teaspoon salt
1 egg, beaten
2 tablespoons parsley, minced
2 drops Tabasco sauce
butter
1 clove garlic, peeled and slightly
    flattened
8 squash or zucchini flowers

Grate squash into a bowl and sift the flour, baking powder, and salt onto it. Mix gently and then mix in the egg, parsley, and Tabasco. Drop from spoon into a little butter and fry as you would any pancake—they should be about 3 inches in diameter. When done, place on a plate and sauté the garlic until it turns golden, then remove it. Flatten the squash flowers with a large knife and quickly sauté them—this takes only a minute or so. Top pancakes with the flowers.
Serves 4–6

This is a bonus recipe for those who have their own gardens. They are great with either morning eggs or an evening chop.

Nopalitos

2 pounds young cactus pads
1 onion slice
1 clove garlic, peeled
2 tablespoons bacon fat (or butter)
2 tablespoons onion, grated
$^1/_2$ cup tomato, chopped
$^1/_2$ teaspoon dried oregano
salt and freshly ground pepper

Hold cactus pads with pliers or kitchen tongs and pull out the thorns with tweezers. Cut into strips the size of green beans and place in a saucepan with onion slice and garlic. Add water to cover, bring to a boil, and simmer 20–30 minutes, or until tender. Drain and discard onion slice and garlic. Heat bacon fat in the saucepan and sauté grated onion for a minute or so, then add tomato, oregano, and salt and pepper to taste. Cook a few minutes, then toss in the cactus and let the mixture heat through.
Serves 4–6

Cactus pads should not be much larger than the palm of your hand to be tender, and they can be found in large Hispanic markets, sometimes with the thorns already removed. In some places you can use prickly pear pads picked fresh from your yard if you can figure out how to avoid wounding yourself on the thorns. Nopalitos have not much flavor but do have a lovely texture like green beans barely cooked. Canned cactus can be used in this recipe; simply omit the preliminary boiling with onion and garlic.

Jicama Sautéed with Coriander

4 cups jicama, peeled and cut in
  ¹/₂-inch dice
2 tablespoons butter
salt
1 clove garlic, minced
1 teaspoon lemon juice (or lime)
2 tablespoons fresh coriander,
  minced (or parsley)

Prepare jicama and put in a bowl of water. When ready to cook, drain it and pat dry with paper towels. Heat butter in a frying pan over high heat, and when it melts add jicama and fry 5 minutes, tossing now and again, until it starts to brown on all sides. Sprinkle with salt to taste, add garlic, and toss another minute. Add lemon, cover, turn heat down low, and cook 10–12 minutes—or until done through but still crisp. Turn heat up high and toss with coriander a minute, then serve.

Serves 4

Jicama is usually served raw as an appetizer, or in salads, but it sautés beautifully. Cooking brings out its flavor without any loss of crispness.

New Mexican Green Beans

1 tablespoon bacon fat (or butter)
1/4 cup green onion, minced with
    part of tops
1 clove garlic, minced
1/2 cup tomatoes, chopped
pinch of ground coriander
1/4 teaspoon powdered red chile (or
    chili powder)
salt
1 pound green beans (fresh or
    frozen)

In a saucepan, sauté onion and garlic in bacon fat over medium heat until softened. Add tomatoes, spices, and salt to taste. When the mixture comes to a boil add the green beans and cook, covered, until crisply tender.

Serves 4

These beans can be either french-cut or cut into 1-inch lengths on the diagonal.

San Antonio Cream Peas

1 tablespoon butter
¹/₄ cup green chile, chopped
¹/₄ teaspoon dried mint
¹/₂ cup cream
salt
1 package frozen tiny peas

Melt butter in a saucepan over medium heat. Add chile and mint, and cook a minute or so to heat through. Add cream and salt to taste and let it almost come to a boil. Remove from heat, place in a blender or food processor, whirl smooth, and put back in the pan. Bring to a boil over high heat and cook down, stirring until reduced and slightly thickened. Put peas in boiling salted water and cook only until the water comes to the boil again. Drain them and put in the cream sauce. Cover, and simmer 1–2 minutes.

Serves 4

Fresh garden peas should only be shown to the fire and quickly buttered, but no one has them all the time, so we must take to frozen. Unfortunately there are few recipes to make the most of this admitted substitute, though this one puts them in quite another light. A teaspoon of minced fresh mint is better than dried, if you have it, and fresh coriander can stand in.

Quelites

2 pounds lamb's-quarters
1 teaspoon bacon fat (or butter)
$^1/_4$ cup onion, chopped
1 green chile, chopped
salt

Discard tough stems of the lamb's quarters. Drop into boiling salted water and cook a minute or so, just to wilt. Drain in a sieve, pressing until all water is out. Melt fat or butter in a saucepan and sauté onion until soft. Add the chile and cook a couple more minutes, then add the lamb's quarters with a little salt and cook until heated through.
Serves 4

Most recipes from the Southwest indicate that spinach is interchangeable with the wild quelites (or lamb's-quarters). I suppose it may be, but there is no substitute for the meaty rich flavor of the real thing.

Corn with Green Chiles

2 cups fresh scraped corn (or 1
 package frozen)
2 tablespoons butter
$1/2$ cup green chile, chopped
$1/4$ teaspoon garlic, minced
salt and freshly ground pepper
pinch of sugar

If you use frozen corn, place it
in boiling water and cook just
until it thaws. Fresh corn only has
to be cut off the cob. Heat butter
in a saucepan and add corn and all
the other ingredients. Cover, and
cook over low heat 10–12
minutes, or until corn is tender.
(It may be necessary to add a little
water during the cooking if the
heat is too high.)
 Serves 4

*Now that we get corn on the cob nearly all year round I hardly ever turn to
frozen, for even if the ear was picked weeks ago it still seems to have more flavor.
This recipe, though, gives a lot of bounce to either.*

Corn Fritters

1 cup corn (preferably freshly
  scraped)
1/4 cup green chiles, chopped
1 tablespoon pimiento, chopped
  (optional)
1/4 cup cornmeal
1 cup flour
1 1/2 teaspoons baking powder
1/2 teaspoon salt
1/4 teaspoon powdered red chile
2 eggs, separated
1/2 cup milk
butter

Place corn, chiles, and pimiento
in a bowl. Add cornmeal, then sift
flour, baking powder, salt and
chile over the corn, mixing well.
Separate eggs and stir yolks and
milk in. Beat egg whites stiff and
fold in carefully. Fry in a little
butter until golden on both sides.
Each fritter should be about 2
inches in diameter.
  Serves 4

*Any corn fritter is a noble dish as far as I am concerned, but those of this
part of the country have the extra bit of chiles to give them new character.*

197

Corn in Red Chile Sauce

$^{1}/_{2}$ cup sour cream
2 tablespoons cream
$^{1}/_{2}$ teaspoon lime juice
1 cup Red Chile Sauce (p. 51)
4 ears of corn, shucked
salt
lime wedges

Blend sour cream, cream, and lime juice so there are no lumps. Let sit 2 hours at room temperature to thicken. Heat chile sauce—it should be fairly thin, and should flow from a spoon easily, so add water if necessary. Put corn in a pot of cold salted water and turn heat on high. The corn is done when the pot comes to a boil; lift immediately out of the water. Spoon chile sauce onto four plates. With a spoon dribble the cream mixture in three vertical lines over the sauce on each plate, then take a knife and run it horizontally through the cream lines so a marbelized pattern is created. Place an ear of corn over the sauce on each plate and garnish with lime wedges. Serve immediately.
Serves 4

I've always thought it beside the point to put anything on a hot ear of garden corn but salt and butter, but this saucing is both a beautiful way to present corn and a delight on the tongue.

Green Corn Cakes in Red Chile Sauce

1³/₄ cups corn, freshly cut (or 1
 package frozen)
2 eggs, separated
1 tablespoon masa harina (or flour)
2 teaspoons cream of tartar
¹/₄ teaspoon salt
2 drops Tabasco sauce
3 tablespoons fresh coriander,
 minced (or parsley)
butter
Red Chile Sauce (p. 51)

Put corn (thawed, if you use
frozen), egg yolks, masa, cream of
tartar, salt, Tabasco, and coriander
into a blender or food processor.
Whirl until the mixture looks like
creamed corn—only a few pulses.
Whip egg whites stiff, but not
dry, and fold corn into them. Heat
a lump of butter in a frying pan
over medium heat. When it
sizzles, fry portions of about ¹/₄
cup of the mixture—spreading it
out to 3-inch cakes—4 minutes a
side. The cakes should be holding
together and lacy golden-brown
before you turn them. Fry all
cakes, adding butter as needed,
and serve in a pool of red chile
sauce.

Serves 4

*For full flavor these ought to have fresh corn, masa, and fresh coriander, but
they are so good they survive very well with the substitutions. Try them as an
accompaniment to plain chops or chicken.*

Chiles Rellenos

6 fresh green chiles, peeled (see Ingredients)
6 slices Cheddar cheese (or Monterey Jack, or Picadillo)
flour
2 eggs, separated
2 tablespoons flour
pinch of salt
oil for frying
1 tablespoon olive oil
1 clove garlic, minced
1/4 cup onion, minced
1 cup canned tomatoes
1 cup chicken stock
salt and freshly ground pepper
1/4 teaspoon dried oregano
pinch of ground cumin

Cut cheese into slices and stuff the chiles (or spoon in about 1/4 cup Picadillo). Roll each in flour. Beat egg whites stiff, but not dry, then fold in yolks which have been lightly beaten. Sift flour and salt over the eggs and fold in carefully. Scoop egg mixture onto a plate and place chiles on top, turning to completely coat with the batter. Pour about an inch of oil in a frying pan and heat (try a pinch of the egg batter to see if it browns immediately). Slip the chiles one by one onto a saucer with as much batter as possible, then push it with a spoon into the oil. When gold on the underside, flip over and cook until gold on the other—about 30 seconds a side. Remove with a slotted spoon to paper towels. To make the sauce put olive oil in a saucepan and sauté onion and garlic until soft. Add tomatoes, stock, a little salt and pepper, and oregano and cumin. Let bubble 10 minutes, then purée in a blender or food processor. Return to a frying pan large enough to hold all the chiles. Bring to a simmer, add chiles, cover, and let them steam 5 minutes, or until puffed up. (They may also be cooked in a 350° oven with the sauce until they puff.)

Serves 3 or 6

Chiles Rellenos are one of my favorite dishes in the world, and I always order them in a new restaurant as a test of the kitchen. Usually a tomato sauce is poured over them immediately after they are cooked, but I prefer this recipe, where they can sit awhile and then be heated in the sauce so there is not the last minute rush. They make a fine addition to a combination platter, along with a taco, an enchilada, and whatnot, and with two or three to a plate they make a lovely supper along with some beans and lettuce garnish. They can be made with whole canned green chiles, but this is one recipe where the fresh chiles really make a difference.

Chiles Rellenos Casserole

4 green chiles, peeled (fresh or canned)
4 slices Cheddar cheese (or Monterey Jack)
4 eggs, separated
¼ cup flour
½ teaspoon salt
Green Chile Sauce (p. 53)

Preheat oven to 400°. Stuff chiles with cheese. Beat egg whites stiff, but not dry. Beat yolks until creamy, and fold into the whites. Sift flour and salt over and fold them in. Place half the egg mixture in a buttered casserole, put chiles on top, then cover with rest of the mixture. Bake 10 minutes, or until the soufflé begins to brown on top. Serve with some sauce ladled over each portion.
Serves 2 or 4

These are nearly as good as regular Chiles Rellenos, and less fattening since they are not fried. They can be served, if you wish, with a tomato sauce rather than the green chile sauce.

Chiles Rellenos with Beans

4 peeled green chiles (fresh or
  canned)
1 cup Refried Beans (p. 60)
flour
2 eggs, separated
2 tablespoons flour
pinch of salt
oil for frying
$^1/_3$ cup cream
$^1/_2$ cup Cheddar cheese, grated (or
  Monterey Jack)
Green Chile Sauce (p. 53)

Preheat oven to 375°. Stuff chiles with beans and roll in flour. Make a batter with the eggs, flour, and salt as in Chiles Rellenos (p. 200), and proceed to cook them as in that recipe. When golden, remove to a baking dish large enough to hold them all in a single layer, pour cream over, sprinkle with cheese, and bake 10 minutes—or until the cheese is melted and the cream bubbles. Serve with sauce ladled over.
  Serves 2

Since this dish has beans, it is not one to be served on a combination platter that already includes beans. It is rather one of those splendid little suppers or lunches to be whipped up using tag ends of another meal. Canned chiles are fine here because the beans don't ooze out of splits as cheese does.

Garbanzo Purée

1 pound dried garbanzos
1 onion
2 carrots
2 slices of bacon
3 cups beef stock
1 bay leaf
$^{1}/_{2}$ teaspoon each dried thyme and
  oregano
2 sprigs parsley
butter
salt

Soak garbanzos overnight in water. Drain, and put in a large pot with onion, carrots, bacon, stock, and herbs. Add enough water to come up 2 inches over the beans. Bring to a boil, lower heat, and simmer 4–5 hours—or until beans are very tender and beginning to fall apart. Drain the garbanzos, reserving the stock. Pick out the vegetables, bacon, and bay leaf, and purée them through a food mill, adding some of the stock, butter, and salt to taste. (They should be thick and creamy, not soupy.) Serve with a lump of butter on top.
Serves 6

Prepared in this manner, garbanzos taste very much like chestnuts, though not so sweet. They are particularly good with lamb and pork dishes, and make a fine stuffing for a turkey on holidays. They look very nice sprinkled with hulled pumpkin seeds.

Saffron Rice with Stuffed Green Chiles

1 cup long grain rice
2½ cups chicken stock
pinch of saffron
salt
4 tablespoons butter, melted
6 whole green chiles (canned or
    fresh)
1 3-ounce package cream cheese

Preheat oven to 350°. Cook rice in stock, saffron, and a little salt if the stock is not salty. It should cook over low heat, covered, 20–25 minutes. Butter a shallow casserole with some of the butter and place the rice in it. Stuff chiles with cream cheese and lay on top. Pour the rest of the butter over, and bake 10–15 minutes—or until the cheese begins to melt.
Serves 6

An unusual and attractive dish which makes a fine accompaniment to chicken or lamb.

Rice with Toasted Piñon Nuts

Cook rice by your favorite method. When done, add a few drops Tabasco sauce and a lump of butter. Mix thoroughly. Toss with piñon nuts which have been sautéed in butter until lightly golden. Serve garnished with parsley.

I'm not a fan of the so-called Spanish Rice so often used to fill out Southwestern platters, but this recipe is a favorite time and again with many dishes, from many cuisines. Piñon nuts are quite expensive in the small packets found in supermarkets (and usually stale, as well). If you are lucky enough to live in the Southwest, there are many outlets for the fresh fall crop. These are relatively inexpensive, bought in bulk, and can be stored in the freezer to keep them sweet tasting. Elsewhere in the country the best place to look for bulk piñon nuts is in a health food store.

Green Rice

2 green bell peppers
1/3 cup parsley
1/4 cup green chiles
1 1/2 cups chicken stock
salt
1 cup long grain rice
1 tablespoon butter
hulled pumpkin seeds

Cut peppers in quarters and remove the seeds. Grate them, flesh side to the coarse part of the grater, until only the tough skin remains. Discard the skins. Place pepper, parsley, and chiles in a measuring cup and press down. Add enough water to make up a cup. Place in a blender or food processor and whirl smooth. Add this to a saucepan with 1 1/2 cups chicken stock. Bring to boil, add rice, salt to taste, and butter. Simmer covered 20 minutes, or until tender and the liquid is absorbed. Serve sprinkled with pumpkin seeds.
Serves 4

This green rice sprinkled with pale green pumpkin seeds is a lovely side dish for fish, chicken, or what have you.

Guacamole Rice Ring

Cook rice in your favorite manner, and when done pack into a well-buttered ring mold. Place the mold in a shallow pan of hot water and bake at 350° 30 minutes. Unmold the ring onto a platter and spread it all over with Guacamole (p. 219). Garnish with parsley and serve.

This makes a nice party dish for a buffet, or you can serve it for family with meatballs or something like Chicken with Green Chiles and Sour Cream (p. 136) in the middle.

Texas Spoonbread

3 cups milk
1 cup cornmeal (preferably stone-
   ground)
1 teaspoon salt
1 teaspoon bacon fat (or butter)
1 teaspoon sugar
1/3 cup green chiles, chopped
1/2 cup Monterey Jack cheese,
   grated
3 eggs, separated

Preheat oven to 350°. Scald milk in a large saucepan. When bubbles begin to form around the edge, whisk in the cornmeal bit by bit. Stir until mixture thickens, then continue cooking over very low heat 5 minutes—stirring now and again to make sure it doesn't stick on the bottom. Add salt, fat, and sugar, and cook several minutes longer. Remove from the heat and stir in chiles, cheese, and egg yolks. Grease a soufflé dish with bacon fat or butter and heat in the oven. Whip whites stiff, but not dry, and fold into the cornmeal mixture. Place in the hot dish and bake 45 minutes, or until puffed up and beginning to brown on top. Serve with butter.

Serves 6

Spoonbread, with or without the chiles and cheese Texans put in it, is one of the glories of American cookery. It is always welcome with any meat dish, simple or sauced.

Tortilla Bread

1 package dry yeast
2 cups lukewarm water
2½ cups unbleached flour
  (approximately)
1 tablespoon brown sugar
2 teaspoon salt
2 cups masa harina
1 4-ounce can mild green chiles,
  chopped

Put yeast in a bowl with ¼ cup of the water and let sit until it puffs. Place in a bowl with the flour, sugar, salt, and the rest of the water. Beat—preferably with an electric mixer—several minutes. Stir in masa, then enough more flour to make a stiff dough. Turn out onto a floured board and knead in the chiles. Knead 5–10 minutes, or until smooth and silky. Place in a greased bowl, and turn well to cover with grease. Let rise, covered with a towel or plastic wrap, in a warm place until doubled, about an hour. Punch down and let rest 15 minutes, then shape into two round loaves. Place in greased pie pans, cover again, and let rise until doubled again. Brush with oil and bake in a preheated 375° oven 30 minutes—or until golden brown on top.

Makes 2 loaves

Though tortillas are the staple bread of the region, other breads are baked and savored. This one has all the taste of fresh tortillas and makes wonderful toast or sandwiches—my favorite filling being Carnitas (p. 144) and thinly sliced sweet onions.

Navajo Fry Bread

2 cups flour
3 teaspoons baking powder
1 teaspoon salt
2 tablespoons vegetable shortening
²/₃ cup hot water
oil for frying

Sift flour, baking powder, and salt into a bowl. Cut in shortening until the mixture resembles meal. Stir in hot water until a dough is formed. Knead a few times on a floured board, gather into a ball, and put in a plastic bag for the dough to rest about 45 minutes. Pinch off pieces of dough about the size of golf balls. Roll them out on a floured board until about 6 inches in diameter. Poke your finger through the center of each round (this will later make a slight depression in the dry bread—otherwise they would puff up into a dome). Pour oil to a depth of 2 inches in a frying pan and heat to about 375°–380°. Fry the breads one at a time until golden brown and crisp on both sides, then drain on paper towels.
Makes 12

Sometimes these are made and dribbled with honey like Sopaipillas (p. 266), but they are much better, I think, served as you would any tostada—with beans, cheese, lettuce, and some Fresh Salsa (p. 55).

Corn and Flour Tortillas

Most Southwestern cookbooks give recipes for making your own tortillas, but as they are so commonly available these days (as well as being inexpensive!) I see no reason to attempt it. They are very difficult to master, even with a tortilla press, I've found, and though the fatter handmade ones are delightful as hot bread, it's impossible to make them thin enough to be good for crisply fried tacos or tostados.

Both corn and flour tortillas are often served as a simple bread at a meal. If they are freshly made that day, all you have to do is wrap them in foil and heat in a moderate oven, then serve in their packet in a basket at table, with butter to spread on them. If they are over a day old, or frozen thawed, sprinkle them with a little water first before wrapping in foil—they will steam and soften beautifully.

Salads

With the usual Guacamole and shredded lettuce seen so commonly on platters, most forget what a fund of interesting and exotic salads the desert states afford. There are all kinds of preparations using avocados in ways other than mashed, spicy variations of the ordinary tossed green salad, as well as ones using unusual ingredients like papaya, jicama, and tomatillo. All are good.

Avocado Slices in Rum

2 avocados, peeled, seeded, and
 sliced
¹/₂ cup olive oil
3 tablespoons lime juice (or white
 wine vinegar)
2 tablespoons rum
1 clove garlic, minced
salt and freshly ground pepper

Combine all the ingredients and marinate, covered, in the refrigerator for an hour or more. (The avocado won't turn dark if all the pieces are well-tossed in the marinade.) Serve fanned out on a plate with a sprig of fresh mint, coriander, or parsley.

Serves 4

One of my most favorite recipes, useful either as a first or salad course—perhaps on a butter-lettuce leaf—or as part of the garnish for a combination. If anything is better than guacamole, this is it.

Avocado and Papaya Salad

lettuce leaves (Boston or butter—
   not iceberg)
1 papaya, peeled and sliced
2 avocados, peeled, seeded, and
   sliced
1/4 cup lime juice
1/3 cup olive oil
4 fresh mint leaves, chopped
salt and freshly ground pepper
pinch of sugar
1/2 teaspoon poppy seeds

Place lettuce on salad plates and alternate papaya and avocado slices on them. Combine the rest of the ingredients thoroughly and pour over. Serve immediately.
Serves 4

This makes a lovely first course for a hot, spicy meal, or part of a buffet party, or an accompaniment to a simple brunch.

Guacamole

2 avocados, peeled and seeded
2 tablespoons lemon juice (or lime)
$1/2$ cup green onions, minced with
    part of tops
1 tomato, peeled and diced
    (optional)
1 small clove garlic, minced
salt
pinch of chili powder
pinch of salt

Mash or chop avocados, sprinkle with lemon juice, and mix in all the other ingredients. (Don't bother at all with tomato unless you have garden ripe.) This can be served immediately, but I like to cover it with plastic wrap and chill in the refrigerator for 30 minutes or so, to gather flavor and mellow. Guacamole should be eaten with tortilla chips.
Serves 4

No two guacamoles are quite alike, even from the same hand, but they all are exquisite providing you don't throw in the contents of the refrigerator. Some like it puréed to a creamy consistency, some like it chunky, some like it with or without tomatoes—but essentially this guacamole is nothing more than avocados with a little onion and garlic and lemon juice. I suspect it is also one of those dishes that should be tasted by the cook, and not left up to a mere recipe.

Green Bean and Avocado Salad

2 corn tortillas, cut in matchstick
  strips
oil for frying
salt
1 pound green beans, French cut
  (fresh or frozen)
1 small red onion
1 avocado, peeled, seeded, and cut
  in dice
oil-and-vinegar dressing
lettuce leaves (Boston or butter—
  not iceberg)

Fry the tortilla strips in hot fat until crisp, drain on paper towels, and lightly salt. Blanch green beans in boiling salted water only until just done—still a bit crisp. Immediately drain in a sieve and run cold water over them from the tap. Pat dry and put in a salad bowl. Peel onion and cut from stem to root, then cut each of the halves in thin slices. Put them in the sieve and run cold water over, then pat dry with paper towels. Add onions to the bowl along with the avocado. Toss with dressing lightly and place on lettuce leaves. Sprinkle with the crisp tortilla strips.
Serves 4

This sounds as though it has to happen like lightning, but tortilla strips can be made ahead, the beans can be refrigerated, and onion slices put in salted icewater—all then tossed at the last minute.

Hot Avocado Salad

2 slices bacon, diced
1¹/₂ tablespoons white wine
  vinegar
1 teaspoon chili powder
pinch of sugar
salt and freshly ground pepper
2 tomatoes, peeled and cut in
  eighths
2 avocados, peeled, seeded and
  sliced
4 green onions, chopped with part
  of tops
5 radishes, sliced
lettuce leaves (Boston or butter—
  not iceberg)

Fry bacon in a frying pan until crisp. Remove with a slotted spoon to paper towels. Add vinegar, chili powder, sugar, and salt and pepper to taste to the bacon fat. Let it boil a minute over medium heat. Add tomatoes, avocados, onions, and radishes and toss quickly and carefully, then place on lettuce, sprinkle with bacon, and serve immediately.

Serves 4

A splendid variation on the Midwestern wilted lettuce salad. It is useful on many occasions—not the least being a simple lunch on its own served with plenty of tortilla chips.

Avocado Mousse

1 envelope plain gelatine
1/2 cup chicken stock
2 cups avocado pulp (about 3
   avocados)
3 tablespoons lemon juice
1 tablespoon finely grated onion
   pulp
2 tablespoons chives, minced
salt
3–4 drops Tabasco sauce
3/4 cup cream, whipped
1/4 teaspoon dry mustard
1/2 cup mayonnaise

Soak gelatine in half the chicken stock. Heat the rest to boiling and add to the gelatine, stirring until dissolved. Cool in the refrigerator until a little thickened—about 30 minutes. Sieve avocados (or purée in a food processor). Place in a bowl, squeeze lemon over, then mix in onion, chives, salt to taste, and Tabasco sauce. Whip cream until it holds soft peaks. Mix dry mustard in the mayonnaise and fold into the cream. Stir gelatine into the avocado mixture, then fold into the cream. Place in a lightly oiled 1 quart mold and chill, covered in plastic wrap, 4–5 hours, or until set. Unmold onto a platter and garnish as you wish.
Serves 8

A lovely company presentation, particularly for a buffet party. I like to mound watercress in the middle and serve it with a simple oil and vinegar dressing with a little grated lime or lemon peel added.

Cauliflower Frosted with Guacamole

1 cauliflower, trimmed
1/2 cup olive oil
1/3 cup white wine vinegar (or 1/4
    cup lemon juice)
1/2 teaspoon powdered red chile
pinch of sugar
salt
lettuce
Guacamole (p. 219)
sliced radishes
almonds, blanched, slivered and
    toasted

Cook cauliflower in boiling salted water until the bottom core can be pierced with a fork—15–20 minutes according to size. Make a dressing of the oil, vinegar, chile, sugar, and salt to taste. Pour this over the drained cauliflower placed head down in a bowl. Cover and refrigerate several hours, turning several times. To serve, place cauliflower on a bed of lettuce and spoon some of the dressing over. Coat completely with guacamole. Decorate with radishes and almonds in a pretty pattern.
Serves 4–6

This makes a very festive to-do indeed of the humble cauliflower. It should be brought out when you want to make a splash.

Avocado and Tomato Aspic

Avocado aspic

1 envelope plain gelatine
1/4 cup cold water
1 cup boiling water
1 teaspoon sugar
2 tablespoons lemon juice
1 cup avocado, sieved
1/2 cup sour cream
1/2 cup mayonnaise
salt and freshly ground pepper
2 drops Tabasco sauce

Soften gelatine in cold water, then pour in boiling water and stir until dissolved. Add sugar and half the lemon juice and chill until slightly thickened—about 30 minutes. Add the rest of the lemon juice to the avocado, then stir in other ingredients. Stir in gelatine and pour into a 2-quart mold. Chill until set.

Tomato aspic

1 envelope plain gelatine
1/4 cup cold water
1³/4 cups tomato juice, boiling
1/2 teaspoon sugar
1 tablespoon lemon juice
salt
dash of Worcestershire sauce

Soften gelatine in cold water, then pour in hot tomato juice and stir until dissolved. Add the other ingredients and let cool about 30 minutes in the refrigerator, or until slightly thick but still pourable. Pour over firm avocado aspic and chill until set. Unmold on a bed of lettuce and serve with mayonnaise or whipped cream flavored with horseradish.
Serves 8–10

If you have a beautiful mold you don't use very often hanging on the wall this is the way to make it count. It's good from holiday feasting to summery barbecues—just slice and eat with tortilla chips.

Tossed Salad with Chile Croutons

3 tablespoons butter
1 clove garlic, peeled and slightly
   flattened
1 teaspoon chili powder
3 slices white bread, trimmed, and
   cut in 1/4-inch dice
salt
mixed salad greens for 4 servings
oil-and-vinegar dressing

Melt butter in a frying pan and stir garlic in it over medium heat until the garlic turns golden. Remove the garlic, add chili powder and toss the bread cubes quickly so all are coated in the butter. Shake and toss until the cubes are golden brown all over, and drain on paper towels. Salt them lightly. Toss salad greens with a light oil-and-vinegar dressing and add croutons on the last toss.

Serves 4

These spicy croutons make a great addition to any simple salad.

Tossed Salad with Avocado Dressing

1 avocado, peeled and seeded
1 clove garlic, minced
1 tablespoon lime juice (or lemon)
1 teaspoon dry white wine
$1/4$ cup sour cream
salt
pinch of chili powder
pinch of sugar (optional)
mixed salad greens for 4 servings

Mash avocado and garlic together, then add all but the greens, and mix well. Place, covered, in the refrigerator for 15 minutes or so, then toss lightly with the greens.
Serves 4

The Southwest has variations of an avocado dressing for salads, but this is one of the most suave.

Tossed Green Salad with Piñon and Green Chile Dressing

mixed salad greens for 6 servings
6 green onions, minced with part
  of tops
$^1/_2$ cup piñon nuts
1 tablespoon vegetable oil
salt
$^1/_2$ cup mayonnaise
1 tablespoon lemon juice
$^1/_2$ clove garlic, minced
$^1/_4$ cup green chiles, chopped
1 tablespoon olive oil
salt
pinch sugar
$^1/_4$ teaspoon dried oregano
pinch ground coriander

Wash and drain lettuce, tearing in bite-size pieces. Add green onions and refrigerate. Sauté nuts in oil, stirring over medium heat until golden. Drain on paper towels and salt lightly. Combine the rest of the ingredients and toss the greens lightly with them. Sprinkle with nuts before serving.

Serves 6

A fine salad with a creamy dressing and crisp nuts for contrast—great with a steak.

Green Chile Salad

8 fresh green chiles, peeled (see
   Ingredients)
²/₃ cup olive oil
¹/₃ cup red wine vinegar
salt and freshly ground pepper
1 garlic clove, peeled and slightly
   flattened
pimiento strips
lettuce leaves (butter or Boston—
   not iceberg)

Prepare chiles and cut them lengthwise in quarters. Marinate with oil, vinegar, salt and pepper to taste, and the garlic clove for several hours in the refrigerator. Drain, and serve on lettuce leaves decorated with a few strips of pimiento.

Serves 4

This is a fine way to test a new crop or brand of green chiles, to see how flavorful or hot they are. Canned chiles can be turned to account this way also, but they won't shine like fresh.

Taco Salad

1 pound lean ground beef
1 clove garlic, minced
$1/2$ cup green chiles, chopped
$1^1/2$ cups tomatoes, chopped
salt and freshly ground pepper
1 cup sour cream
2 tablespoons lemon juice
salt
$1/4$ teaspoon ground cumin
6 corn tortillas
oil for frying
1 head iceberg lettuce, torn in
  bite-size pieces
1 cup Cheddar cheese, grated
$1/2$ cup green onions, chopped with
  part of tops
1 avocado, sliced

Add beef and garlic to a frying pan and cook, stirring to break up the meat, until it no longer shows pink. Drain on paper towels, and return to the pan. Add chile, tomatoes (along with juices if you use canned), and salt and pepper to taste. Cook over low heat 30 minutes, adding a little water if necessary. By the time the mixture is cooked there should be no liquid. While meat mixture cooks, make the dressing: combine sour cream, lemon juice, salt, and cumin. Cut tortillas in half, stack the halves, and cut in $1/2$-inch strips. Fry crisp in oil and sprinkle with salt as they drain on paper towels. Just before serving arrange lettuce, cheese, tortilla strips and onion in a salad bowl. Add meat mixture and toss lightly. Top with sour cream dressing and slices of avocado.

Serves 6

A prime luncheon dish. It has all the ingredients of a taco, but they are arranged differently. And this recipe is only a guideline as to what might constitute your salad. Radishes are nice, as well as jicama or cut fresh tomatoes if you have ripe ones, and the cheese can be anything you have on hand. For a fancier presentation you can fry a large flour tortilla in hot oil, holding it down with tongs in the middle, to make a crisp cup for the salad.

Stuffed Green Chile Salad

12 fresh green chiles, peeled (see Ingredients)
1/4 cup red wine vinegar
1/3 cup olive oil
salt
1 cup yellow summer squash, diced
salt and freshly ground pepper
1 clove garlic, minced
1/2 teaspoon dried basil
pinch sugar
2 avocados, peeled and seeded
lettuce leaves
sliced ripe olives

Prepare chiles and marinate in vinegar, oil, and a bit of salt for several hours. Cook squash until barely tender in a little water with salt, pepper, garlic, basil, and a speck of sugar. Drain and chill. To serve the salad, mash avocados with 1 tablespoon of the marinade. Toss with the squash and stuff drained chiles with the mixture. Place on lettuce leaves and decorate with olive slices.

Serves 6

A wonderful first course for an important meal. It is very pretty to look at, and tastes even better.

Tomatillo Salad

12 fresh tomatillos
12 cherry tomatoes, sliced
1 cucumber, peeled and sliced
6 green onions, chopped with part
   of tops
oil and vinegar dressing

Remove husks from tomatillos and slice them. Toss with rest of the ingredients and refrigerate for an hour or so before serving.
Serves 4

Those lucky enough to find tomatillos in their market will delight in this tart, lively salad. Canned tomatillos are too mushy and acid to use here.

Tomatoes Stuffed with Celery and Piñon Nuts

Take medium-ripe garden tomatoes and place each for a minute in boiling water. Then slip skins off, slice the tops off, and squeeze out seeds and pulp. Sprinkle inside with a little salt and invert on paper towels. Let stand 30 minutes to drain. Mix very finely chopped celery and piñon nuts in a three-to-one proportion, with enough good mayonnaise to bind. Stuff tomatoes and serve garnished with parsley.

Store-bought tomatoes are so inedible these days that I only buy them in summer at farmer's markets. But those who have a garden full of the beauties will find this dish a friend again and again. The different crunches of celery and piñon are irresistible.

Green Garbanzo Salad

1 15½-ounce can garbanzos,
  drained
3 green onions, minced with part
  of tops
1 tablespoon parsley, minced
2 tablespoons fresh coriander,
  minced
2 tablespoons green chile, chopped
2–3 tomatillos, chopped (fresh or
  canned)
1 green bell pepper, grated (see
  Ingredients)
1 clove garlic, minced
salt and freshly ground pepper
1 teaspoon grated lime peel (or
  lemon)
2 tablespoons olive oil
1 tablespoon white wine vinegar

Place garbanzos in a bowl.
Prepare the rest of the ingredients
(a food processor is the best of
friends for this) and add to the
garbanzos. Toss, and chill several
hours before serving.
Serves 4–6

A fine dish for outdoor barbecues.

Rooster's Bill

1 small jicama, peeled and cut in
 ¼-inch × 2-inch strips
oil-and-vinegar dressing
Tabasco sauce
chili powder
6 seedless oranges, peeled and
 sliced
6 green onions, minced with part
 of tops

Prepare jicama and toss with dressing, Tabasco, and a good dash of chili powder. Refrigerate for an hour or so. To serve, place orange slices in a fan on salad plates, top with jicama, and sprinkle with green onions.
 Serves 4–6

I used to serve Rooster's Bill (pico de gallo) *with just oranges and onion until I was able to get jicama to make it properly, but even without jicama it makes a fine salad to begin a brunch.*

Desserts

In this section of the country cakes and pies give way to puddings, and exotic fruits such as guavas, mangoes, coconuts, bananas, avocados, and pineapple are fried, moussed, and souffléd with abandon. The principal reason for this is that after a typically spicy Southwestern meal only the lightest or most soothing dessert seems possible—the bland custard, perky ice, or a simple plate of fruit paste with cream cheese. They do have some heavies, usually reserved for holidays, such as the bread pudding called capirotada, that is laced with raisins, nuts, and cheese, all held together with an incredible amount of cinnamon-flavored brown-sugar syrup—a truly awful sweet. But I've excluded those monsters in favor of ones that end a Southwestern meal on a grace note.

Mexican Cream with Strawberries

1 tablespoon plain gelatine
2 cups cream
¹/₂ cup sugar
2 cups sour cream
1 teaspoon vanilla
strawberries

Put gelatine, cream, and sugar in a saucepan. Cook over medium low heat, stirring until gelatine and sugar are dissolved—don't let it boil. Place in a bowl, cover, and refrigerate an hour, or until thickened to the consistency of egg whites. Stir in sour cream and vanilla. Lightly oil a 1¹/₂-quart ring mold, add the cream mixture, cover, and chill until firm—about 6 hours. To serve, run a knife around the mold, dip outside of mold in hot water a few seconds, and invert on a serving plate. Garnish with plenty of fresh strawberries in the center, and around the cream.

Serves 8–10

A delicious cooling dessert, not too sweet, after a hot spicy meal. It is the ideal choice for company, when you want something easy to prepare ahead and pretty to look at.

Flan

1¼ cups sugar
3 cups milk
4 eggs
pinch of salt
1 teaspoon vanilla extract

Preheat oven to 325°. Melt ³/4 cup sugar in a saucepan over medium heat until there are no lumps and it has turned a deep amber. Immediately remove from heat and pour into custard cups or a baking dish. Quickly tip cups or dish in all directions so the sugar coats sides and bottom. Scald milk, and when bubbles begin to come to the sides, remove from heat. Beat eggs frothy and stir in remaining ¹/2 cup sugar, salt, and vanilla. Add scalded milk slowly, beating constantly, then pour through a sieve into cups or baking dish. Set in a pan with about 1 inch hot water in it and bake an hour, or until a knife inserted in the center comes out

clean. (Cups will take less time than a whole custard.) Remove to a rack, cool, then refrigerate covered for several hours. To unmold, run a knife around the edge and invert onto a plate. If you bake as a whole custard, place a platter over the dish, and quickly lift both together and invert.
    Serves 6

Flan is the most usual dessert served after a meal in the Southwest. It is smooth and satisfying after a hot repast, and hard to beat.

Pumpkin Flan

1²/₃ cups sugar
1 cup cream
2 cups milk
2 cups strained pumpkin (fresh
    cooked or canned)
1 teaspoon salt
¹/₂ cup rum
6 eggs

Preheat oven to 350°. Melt 1 cup sugar over medium heat until there are no lumps and it turns a deep amber. Immediately remove from heat and pour into a baking dish. While it is still liquid, tip the dish in all directions quickly so the sugar coats sides and bottom. Scald cream and milk, and when bubbles begin to come to the sides, stir in pumpkin, remaining ²/₃ cup sugar, salt, and rum. Remove from heat. Beat eggs frothy. Pour a bit of the pumpkin mixture into the eggs and beat again. Then add eggs to pumpkin, beating constantly. Pour into the caramelized dish and put it in a pan in which there is about 1 inch of hot water. Bake 1 hour, or until a knife inserted in the center comes out clean. Allow to cool and invert on a serving dish.

Serves 6

This can be served chilled, or still warm and flaming with rum. To flambé, invert and let stand about 10 minutes. Pour off the caramel syrup around the edges into a sauceboat. Warm 1/3 cup rum, pour over flan, and ignite with a match. Keep spooning rum onto the top as it burns to make sure the flame burns itself out. Serve the additional syrup separately.

Coconut Flan

1 cup sugar
6 tablespoons cornstarch
¹/₄ teaspoon salt
3 cups milk
1 cup cream
2 egg yolks
2 cups flaked coconut
1 teaspoon grated orange rind
2 teaspoons vanilla extract
whipped cream

Sift sugar, cornstarch, and salt into the top of a double boiler, then add milk and cream, beating with a whisk until smooth. Cook over boiling water until thickened, stirring occasionally to keep smooth. Beat egg yolks in a bowl and gradually add the hot mixture, beating constantly. Return to the double boiler and cook, stirring steadily, a few more minutes. Cool. Beat with an eggbeater 2 minutes, then fold in coconut, orange rind, and vanilla. Pour into custard cups and chill several hours. Serve with lightly sweetened whipped cream.
Serves 6

A pleasant textured custard—not really a flan though it is named so.

Quick Chocolate Rum Mousse

1¹/₂ cups light cream (or half & half)
5 egg yolks
1¹/₂ cups semi-sweet chocolate chips
pinch of salt
3 tablespoons dark rum
whipped cream

Put cream in a saucepan and scald over medium heat. Be careful not to let it boil over, but just let it get bubbles around the edge. Drop egg yolks in a blender or food processor, add chips, salt, and rum. Pour cream in while blending or processing. Pour into a bowl, cover with plastic wrap, and refrigerate 4–6 hours, or until the mousse has thickened. Serve in scoops on a dessert plate with lightly whipped cream.

Serves 4

At first this seems a slightly dopey recipe that couldn't possibly be worth trying even if it does take only a few minutes. In fact, it makes a fine, rich, dark dessert. The only problem with it is that guests invariably ask for the recipe, and you have to blush to say you cheated. Be sure to use real chocolate chips, though. I use Nestle, which seem to be the best commonly available.

Natillas

2 cups milk
3 eggs, separated
¹/₂ cup sugar
2 tablespoons cornstarch
¹/₈ teaspoon salt
1 teaspoon vanilla
2 sticks cinnamon (or ground
   cinnamon)

Put milk in a saucepan and bring it just to a boiling point. While it heats, separate eggs in this manner: place 3 yolks and one white in one bowl, and 2 whites in another for use later. Beat yolks until light and frothy. Combine sugar, cornstarch, and salt, and beat into the yolk mixture. Pour a bit of hot milk into mixture, then a little more, beating with each addition. Beat the whole into the milk. Cook in a double boiler set over simmering water until thickened—about 10 minutes. Stir as it cooks. Remove from fire, and let cool to room temperature. Stir now and then so a skin doesn't form on top. When cooled stir in vanilla. Whip the reserved whites until they hold a soft peak. Fold into the custard, but stop before they are completely folded—there should be pockets of beaten egg whites and pockets of custard.

Scoop into serving dishes and chill an hour or more. To serve, break cinnamon sticks in half and stick in puddings—or sprinkle with ground cinnamon.

Serves 4

Most natillas are simply a floating-island-type dessert, but this Albuquerque variation gives it an extra twist I find irresistible.

Almendrado

Gelatine mixture

1 tablespoon plain gelatine
1/2 cup cold water
1 cup boiling water
1 cup sugar
5 egg whites
1/2 teaspoon almond extract
1/2 teaspoon vanilla extract

Soak gelatine in cold water until soft, then add boiling water and stir until dissolved. Add sugar and continue stirring until sugar is also dissolved. Chill until it begins to stiffen—about an hour—then remove and beat with an egg beater or electric mixer until frothy. Clean beater and dry thoroughly. Beat egg whites stiff, then fold with almond and vanilla into gelatine mixture. Pour into loaf pan and chill several hours.

Custard sauce

2 cups milk
5 egg yolks
1/4 cup sugar
pinch of salt
1/2 teaspoon almond extract
1/2 teaspoon vanilla extract
chopped, toasted almonds

Scald the milk. Beat yolks in a bowl until light, then beat in sugar and salt. Add a bit of milk, beating well, then add rest of the milk slowly, beating all the while. Put in top of a double boiler, and cook over simmering water until the custard coats the back of a spoon. Remove from fire and add flavorings. Chill. To serve, cut slices of the chilled gelatine mixture, ladle some custard sauce over, and sprinkle with chopped almonds.
Serves 8

Almendrado is popular in some parts of the Southwest as a company dessert. Often the gelatine mixture is divided in three parts, with two colored red and green with food coloring. These are then chilled in layers to resemble the Mexican flag when it is cut—a little gaudy to my mind, but easy enough to do if you want.

Mango Floating Island

3 eggs
1/4 cup sugar
pinch of salt
2 cups milk, scalded
1 tablespoon sherry
1 18-ounce can mangoes
1/2 cup cream
1/4 teaspoon vanilla extract
powdered sugar

Beat eggs in a bowl until light and frothy. Add sugar and salt and mix well. Add milk bit by bit, beating as you go. Cook in the top of a double boiler over simmering water until the mixture coats the back of a spoon. This will take 7–8 minutes. Add sherry and cool the mixture. Drain juices from mangoes and slice. Place in the bottom of a glass serving dish and top with the custard. Chill in the refrigerator several hours. To serve, top with whipped cream flavored with vanilla and powdered sugar to taste.

Serves 4–6

Mangoes make a simple custard into a delicious dessert fit for any company.

Avocado Soufflé

butter
sugar
2 tablespoons butter
3 tablespoons flour
3/4 cup milk, heated
4 egg yolks
1/3 cup sugar
1 teaspoon grated lime peel
2 tablespoons lime juice
1 teaspoon vanilla extract
1 tablespoon rum
3/4 cup sieved ripe avocado
5 eggs whites
pinch of salt
1 tablespoon sugar

Preheat oven to 400°. Butter a 6-cup soufflé dish and sprinkle with sugar to coat. Melt 2 tablespoons butter in a saucepan over medium heat. Stir in flour and cook a few minutes. Add milk all at once and stir until thickened and coming to a boil. Stir 30 seconds, then remove from fire and cool a bit. Stir in yolks, sugar, lime peel and juice, vanilla, rum, and avocado. Beat whites with salt until they hold soft peaks. Beat in sugar, then fold into avocado mixture. Turn into dish and smooth the top. Place in oven and turn heat down to 375°. Bake 30–35 minutes, or until puffed way up. Serve immediately. It's nice to accompany this with lightly whipped cream flavored with a hint of rum.
Serves 6

A soufflé isn't really all that tricky, but it must be served immediately. For that reason I usually cook them only for family—even this luscious avocado triumph.

Guava Paste with Cream Cheese

Serve equal portions of guava paste and softened cream cheese, along with coffee.

Guava paste is available in Hispanic markets, and is good to have on hand for special occasions. It makes the simplest dessert of all, but always welcome.

Quince Cheese

5 pounds quinces
5 pounds sugar

Peel quinces well—they have a quite tough skin. Quarter them and cut out seeds. Place in a large pot, cover with water, and cook until soft, about 30 minutes. Put through a food mill (or whirl in a food processor). Return to the pan and add sugar. Cook over low heat until thick and dark rosy red. Stir frequently to prevent scorching on the bottom. Pour into small molds—custard cups are fine. Cool them, remove from molds, and wrap in cheese cloth. Set in the sun to dry, if necessary bringing in at night, then placing them again in the sun. When dry, wrap in waxed paper and store in an airtight container. Serve with softened cream cheese.

An old recipe from when quinces were more available. But some folks still have a proud old quince tree in the yard, and know what a lovely fruit it is for jellies and preserves. This is another way to use up a crop, similar to, but perhaps even better than Guava Paste.

Mangoes in Orange Sauce

¹/₂ cup sugar
¹/₄ cup water
¹/₄ cup orange juice
¹/₂ teaspoon grated orange rind
3 tablespoons orange liqueur
4 ripe mangoes, peeled and sliced
(or 1 18-ounce can)

Combine sugar, water, orange juice and rind, and liqueur in a saucepan and cook 5 minutes over high heat—or until it makes a syrup. (If you use canned mangoes omit the sugar and water and substitute the can juices.) Pour over mangoes and refrigerate, covered, for a day or more.

Serves 4

These are very good as is, but they also make a delightful topping for vanilla ice cream.

Bananas in Rum

4 bananas
2 tablespoons butter
¹/₃ cup sugar
¹/₃ cup rum

Peel bananas, slice lengthwise, then cut slices in the middle to make 16 finger-shaped slices. Melt butter in a large frying pan set over medium heat. Fry bananas 3 minutes per side, and lift out to a shallow dish large enough to hold them all in one layer. Add sugar and rum to the frying pan and cook, stirring until the sugar dissolves and bubbles. Pour over bananas, cover, and refrigerate several hours. To serve, place bananas in a fan on serving plates. Pour sauce into a saucepan and heat it, then pour over the cold bananas. This can be served, if you wish, with a dollop of whipped cream lightly sugared and flavored with vanilla.
Serves 4

A longtime favorite easy dessert, but one so good it can be served even with a fine French meal.

Bananas Glazed with Guava

¹/₂ cup guava jelly
2 tablespoons rum (or tequila)
6 bananas
3 tablespoons butter
1 teaspoon brown sugar
pinch of salt

Put jelly in a small saucepan and stir it with rum over medium heat until it thickens and is smooth. Slice bananas lengthwise. Melt butter in a frying pan and sauté bananas over medium heat about 2 minutes per side. Add sugar and the barest sprinkle of salt, then turn bananas to glaze. Place on warm plates and pour the guava-rum mixture over.
Serves 6

Guava jelly is not available at the ordinary corner market, but in large stores there are several brands at hand which are dark and tart and delicious to have on the shelf for this or other uses. It is particularly good in recipes that call for a glaze of currant jelly.

Pineapple in White Wine

1 ripe pineapple
$^1/_2$ cup sugar
$1^1/_2$ cups dry white wine
fresh mint sprigs (optional)

Trim pineapple well and cut in $^1/_2$-inch slices. Cut the slices in sixths, and cut out the woody core of each piece. Place in a glass bowl with sugar and wine, and chill in the refrigerator for several hours. Serve garnished with mint.
Serves 6

The flavor of fresh pineapple is perhaps one of the best of all to clear the palate of chiles and spices.

Orange Slices with Avocado Cream

4 oranges
2 tablespoons sugar
2 tablespoons rum
2 large avocados
²/₃ cup sugar
3 tablespoons lime juice
¹/₄ cup cream
pinch of salt

Peel oranges and remove all the white pith. Slice ¹/₄ inch thick and place slices in a bowl with sugar and rum. Cover and refrigerate 2 hours. Peel avocados and purée in a blender or food processor. Add sugar bit by bit as they purée, then whirl with lime, cream, and salt. Cover and also refrigerate 2 hours. To serve, make a circle of oranges on a plate and place a dollop of avocado cream in the center.

Serves 4–6

An almost tropical fantasy to end a meal hot with chiles and spices.

Cantaloupe Ice

1¹/₄ cups sugar
1¹/₄ cups water
1 large ripe cantaloupe
1 tablespoon lemon juice

Place sugar and water in a saucepan and stir them over high heat until the mixture begins to bubble and sugar is dissolved. Simmer 5 minutes. Place in a jar and refrigerate until cool. Peel and seed the cantaloupe and cut into cubes. Purée in a blender or food processor (this should make 3¹/₂ cups purée). Add lemon juice and syrup. Freeze in a machine according to directions, or freeze in trays 30 minutes before serving, blend or process again, and put back in the freezer to firm.
Serves 4–6

Cantaloupe is perhaps my favorite sherbet after a heavy meal. If the melon is ripe and flavorful you will have a dessert better than most any sherbet you could buy. It can also be adapted for other melons if you measure 3¹/₂ cups of purée.

Avocado Sherbet

1 cup sugar
1 1/2 cups water
3 medium avocados
2/3 cup lemon juice (or lime)
1 teaspoon lemon rind, grated (or lime)

Put sugar and water in a saucepan and stir over high heat until the sugar is dissolved. Turn heat low and simmer 5 minutes. Place in a jar and refrigerate till cool. Peel and pit the avocados and purée in a blender or food processor. Add lemon juice and rind, and the syrup. Freeze in a machine according to manufacturer's directions, or freeze in ice trays, whirling in a blender or processor 30 minutes before serving, and placing back in the freezer to firm.
Serves 4

If you can resist serving avocados or guacamole in your meal, then count on this velvety delight to end it.

Mexican Chocolate Ice Cream

1 ounce unsweetened chocolate
1/4 teaspoon cinnamon
2/3 cup sugar
3/4 cup water
3 egg whites
1 1/2 teaspoons vanilla extract
2 cups cream

Grate chocolate and blend with cinnamon. Put sugar and water in a saucepan, bring to a boil, and let simmer 5 minutes. Beat whites stiff and gradually beat the sugar syrup into them, then immediately beat in the chocolate mixture and vanilla. Whip cream till it holds soft peaks and fold it in. Freeze in ice trays. A half-hour before serving, place ice cream in a food processor or blender and whirl smooth. Place back in the freezer to firm up.
Serves 4–6

In Mexico (and the Southwest too) a little cinnamon is always mixed with chocolate to make it sing.

Mango Ice with Rum Mango Topping

2 cups mangoes, puréed
1¹/₂ cups powdered sugar
¹/₂ cup water
1 lemon, juiced
3 mangoes, peeled and cut in
   cubes
2 tablespoons rum
¹/₄ cup powdered sugar

Combine the mango purée, powdered sugar, water, and lemon juice. Freeze in a machine according to manufacturer's directions. Or freeze in ice trays and run through a blender or food processor 30 minutes before serving, then place back in freezer to firm. While the ice is being made combine mango cubes, rum, and sugar, and chill in the refrigerator. Serve ice with rum mangoes on top.
Serves 6

A lovely exotic dessert that can also be made with canned mangoes if you can't find fresh. In that case, though, use half as much sugar in the ice and add the juice from the can. Add no sugar to the topping. When buying mangoes look for those that are well colored rather than green, and are slightly soft to the touch.

Tequila Sherbet

1¹/₂ cups sugar
3 cups water
¹/₂ teaspoon grated lime peel
¹/₂ cup lime juice
¹/₃ cup tequila
1 egg white
¹/₄ teaspoon salt

Place sugar and water in a saucepan, bring to a boil, and simmer 5 minutes. During the last minute of cooking add lime peel. Remove from fire and stir in lime juice. Place in freezer in ice trays and freeze to a thick mush. Remove and place in a blender or food processor. Whirl with tequila, egg white, and salt. Freeze again, and blend again before serving. If too mushy, place back in the freezer 30 minutes to firm.
Serves 4

This is rather like a margarita, but with less tequila. Don't be tempted to add more tequila, though, because the addition of more alcohol will keep the mixture from freezing.

Cinnamon Crisps

flour tortillas
oil for frying
sugar
cinnamon

Cut tortillas in six pie-shaped wedges. Fry until crisp in hot oil, drain on paper towels, and shake in a bag of cinnamon sugar (in the proportion of $1/2$ cup sugar to 1 teaspoon cinnamon).

Children love these as snacks, and they are a fine way to use up flour tortillas that are going stale. They also make a nice, crisp garnish to fruit ices, or compotes.

Guava Empanadas

4 flour tortillas
7 ounces guava paste (or any jam)
3 ounces cream cheese (or yoghurt)
oil for frying
powdered sugar

Moisten edges of the tortillas; they should be very fresh if possible. Place $1/2$-inch slices of guava paste on one side of each tortilla, and top with slices of cream cheese. Fold the tortillas over the filling like a turnover, and press moist edges firmly together with tines of a fork to seal. Fry in at least 1 inch hot oil (about 350°), about 3 minutes per side. Lift out onto paper towels to drain, then sprinkle with powdered sugar. Eat while warm.
Serves 4

Empanadas are usually made from a pastry dough that, frankly, often is quite heavy after being fried. These beauties use flour tortillas, which are always light and crispy, and they make a dessert easily put together after a simple supper or lunch (though they are perhaps a bit much after a complex dinner). You can use any jam at hand and some yoghurt for a lighter, more accessible version your kids will clamor for.

Sopaipillas

2 cups flour
1½ teaspoons baking powder
1 teaspoon salt
2 tablespoons vegetable shortening
  (or lard)
²⁄₃ cup hot water
oil for frying
powdered sugar
honey

Sift flour, baking powder, and salt into a bowl. Cut shortening in until the mixture resembles meal, then stir in hot water with a fork until the mixture makes a dough. Knead a couple of times on a lightly floured surface, then gather into a ball and keep in a plastic bag 45 minutes at room temperature. Roll out dough on a lightly floured surface to ¼-inch thickness. Cut in 3-inch squares. Put oil in a pan to about the depth of 2 inches and heat to 375–380°. Fry a few of the squares at a time, spooning hot oil over them to help puffing. Drain on paper towels and sprinkle powdered sugar over. Serve warm, to be split open and have honey dribbled in.
Makes 18

I've never much liked sopaipillas with a meal or as a dessert—they seem too heavy for rich food. But I had them once with hot breakfast chocolate, turned out in crisp batches, and found them perfect.

Biscochitos

1/2 pound lard
3/4 cup sugar
1 egg
2 tablespoons brandy (or bourbon)
3 cups flour
1 1/2 teaspoons baking powder
1/2 teaspoon salt
1 teaspoon anise seeds
1/4 cup sugar
1/2 teaspoon cinnamon

Preheat oven to 350°. In a large bowl, cream lard and sugar until light and fluffy. Beat in egg and brandy. Sift flour, baking powder, and salt together and beat in bit by bit. Then beat in anise seeds. Roll the batter out about 1/8 inch thick on a lightly floured surface. Cut with a biscuit cutter, or into fancy cookie shapes. Combine sugar and cinnamon and sprinkle tops of the cookies. Bake on lightly greased sheets for about 10 minutes, or until just beginning to take on color. When cool, store in a tight container—they will keep for weeks.

Makes 6 dozen 1 3/4-inch cookies.

A great cookie to have on hand for serving with fruits, ices, or puddings. They can be made with vegetable shortening rather than lard, but I think lard gives a better flavor.

Polvorones

2 cups unsalted butter, at room
   temperature
1 cup walnuts or pecans, finely
   chopped
2 cups flour
$1/2$ cup powdered sugar
pinch salt
2 tablespoons rum
powdered sugar

Preheat oven to 350°. Beat butter in a mixer until quite soft. The nuts should be very finely chopped—the easiest way to do this is to put them with a cup of the flour in a blender or food processor, then whirl until fine. Add all the ingredients bit by bit to the butter, mixing after each addition. Roll into balls the size of a walnut, flatten slightly, and place on ungreased cookie sheets. Bake 12–15 minutes, or until palest gold. Cool 5 minutes, then lift from sheets and dredge in more powdered sugar. Store in an airtight tin.

Makes 5 dozen

These cookies melt as you eat them. Nice with coffee, they are also great partners for any ice or creamy dessert.

Ingredients

Avocados   There are several different kinds of avocado on the market, the most common being the Hass (small, with a black pebbly skin) and the Fuerte (green and smooth). The Hass has a better flavor, I think— particularly for desserts. They are ready to eat when they yield to a gentle poke.

Beans   There are many excellent beans used in Mexico which are unheard-of and unavailable in this country. Pinto beans and kidney beans are the most common varieties here, and both are used, often interchangeably, in the Southwest. I grow ever fonder, though, of black beans, which take a little hunting for, but are usually available at Hispanic markets. They have a rich, dark flavor and can be used anywhere pinto beans are called for here. For dried beans I have usually indicated that they should be soaked in water overnight, but the short-soak method of bringing them to a boil for a few minutes, then steeping covered for an hour before starting to cook is fine. (Actually if you buy fresh dried beans in bulk they really don't need any preliminary soaking.) Canned beans can, of course, be used for those in a rush, but they never have as much flavor. Try cooking them with a bit of onion, a slice of bacon, a clove of garlic, and a pinch of chili powder or small dried chiles, for a better flavor.

Cheese   Cheeses are now being produced in California and the Southwest that are more like the white crumbly product of Mexico, but these are not widely available in most parts of the country. I've relied here on Cheddar, which can be mild or sharp as you choose, and on the creamy mild Monterey Jack, which should always have "natural" on the label or it will tend to be stringy when melted. Many Southwesterners swear by longhorn cheese, and indeed it is usually a fairly acceptable cheese in the Southwest, but in most of the rest of the country it is sold

269

too green and rubbery to be of much help, for it has little flavor and tends to glue as it melts—use a mild Cheddar instead. There is no excuse for "processed" cheese.

Chiles These come in many shapes and sizes and degrees of hotness, and they can be confusing even to the knowledgeable since their names are switched about from place to place. I suggest anyone who cooks this cuisine often become acquainted with all the fresh and dried chiles available in whatever region they find themselves. For simplicity I have here limited recipes to chiles easily available everywhere: the dried red New Mexico chile, the mild green Anaheim chile, which can be either fresh or canned, and the pickled Jalapeño, which is usually labeled "bottled en escabeche." I myself prefer a wide choice of chiles and keep nearly a dozen varieties, both fresh and dried, on hand.

Green Chiles The most common varieties are the Anaheim (mild, long, bright green) and the Poblano (medium hot, wide and large, dark green, rich in flavor). To prepare fresh chiles either hold on a long fork over a flame or place under a broiler until the chiles are blistered black all over. Seal them in a paper bag as they cook—this allows them to steam and further loosen the skins. The best way to get the skins off is to scrape and brush under running water. The stems, seeds, and rib veins should be cut out before using, as these are the hottest part of the chile. Fresh chiles are, as you can see, rather a bother, but are always preferable to canned if you have time and energy. In the Southwest they are available frozen, but the rest of us must make do.

Red Chiles These are the ripe and dried form of green chiles—called Ancho, California, or New Mexico. They range from bright brick red to deep, ruddy brown (and even black, if you can find the Chile Negro).

270

There are a variety of ways to prepare them, but they should always be stemmed, seeded, and deveined before cooking, as the seeds and veins are hotter than hot. In some parts of the country you can find ground red chile (referred to in this book as red chile powder and not to be confused with chili powder, the commercial product including garlic, cumin, oregano, and whatnot). Red chile powder can be substituted for red chiles at about 2 teaspoons per chile. Some people always roast their chiles in a low oven before using, which gives a deeper flavor to a sauce, but is not absolutely necessary. Also, always check a new batch of chiles by boiling one in a little water, then tasting the cooking liquid and skin—if bitter, do not use the liquid or skins to make a sauce, but rub them through a sieve and use only the pulp.

Small Chiles The Jalapeño is very hot—the smaller the hotter, in fact. They are 1–2 inches long and dark bright green, though sometimes you will find them ripe red. In their fresh state they give a lively flavor to salsa, and particularly to egg dishes. I have used only the pickled jalapeño here, because it is so widely available, but fresh are great to experiment with. The Serrano is similar in size and shape, but smaller and lighter green. They have a superior flavor, but are also very hot. Guero are yellow, quite hot, and about the shape and size of a Jalapeño. They can be used interchangeably with either Jalapeño or Serrano. Arbol and Japones are small dried red chiles, great as an addition to beans as they cook, or in most stews, but as they are very hot I wouldn't recommend they be added to just any dish. The most potent of the small dried reds are the Chile Pequin or Tepin. They are tiny round ovals, and are good either in cooking beans, or as a fiery touch to a Salsa.

Chili powder For some reason chile in this form is always spelled chili—confusing, but I have followed the practice in order to differentiate it from pure ground red chile powders. It is good to shop around for the best chili powder—some are milder and some more complex. The most common ingredients in them are cumin, garlic, oregano, cloves, and allspice. If you have access to fine red chile powder you can add all these on your own, to balance dishes differently—more cumin for one, a speck of cloves for another.

Chorizo   This is the Mexican or Spanish sausage. It is available in many markets, but even so I prefer to use the recipe for it given here, as it is easily prepared, easy to keep frozen in batches, and is superior to even the best of the commercial varieties (some of which are full of fat and gristle and indifferent spices). If you are using store-bought chorizo sold as link sausage, however, you have only to take off the casing to use it as these recipes indicate.

Coriander   This fresh herb is also known as cilantro—and sometimes as Chinese parsley. It used to be found only in Chinese or Hispanic markets, but is now becoming more and more widely available. Its use makes the main difference in my own cooking of Southwestern foods since I first acquired a taste for it ten years ago, and I put it in nearly every fresh or cooked sauce, use it with many a meat, and also as a sprightly garnish. It has a very pungent fragrance and flavor, and it makes the special difference in so many dishes I recommend you try it. If not available in your market, it is easy to grow from the coriander seeds sold in the spice counter of every store. It needs medium to heavy soil in a sunny location with good drainage and moisture. The plants take 3–4 months to mature. Dried coriander leaves are tasteless, but you can purée the leaves with some oil and freeze them in small batches—ice cube trays are perfect. In cooking, only the leaves are used, and the dried seeds. In any dish that calls for fresh coriander it's nice to add a little ground coriander as well—though they have very different tastes, they combine to boost one another.

Garbanzos   These are also known as chick-peas and are available anywhere. They take a long time to cook, longer than most any other dried bean, but canned garbanzos are quite acceptable to save time here, as there is very little difference in taste between fresh cooked and canned. Two large cans are about the equivalent of a pound of cooked dried.

Green bell peppers   The ordinary sweet pepper found everywhere, and of the same family as hot chiles. I use it often to perk up the flavor of canned green chiles. Rather than go to the trouble of roasting and peeling them, though, I have developed a method of grating which uses only the flavorful flesh and discards tough skin. Simply quarter and core the pepper and grate it with the flesh against the coarse side of a grater—its skin will remain and can be discarded.

Herbs   There are very few dishes in Southwestern cooking where fresh herbs are absolutely necessary, but certainly if you grow your own these are always preferable. Use 1 tablespoon fresh for 1 teaspoon dried.

Jicama   A sweetly crisp tuber reminiscent of water chestnuts. Wonderful for appetizers, salads, and even cooked as a vegetable. It has a very tough rind that must be peeled right down to the white flesh before using. Jicama is becoming more and more widely available—look for it in your market. It looks like a huge, rough, brown turnip.

Lamb's-quarters   Known as *quelites* or *epazote* more often than not in

the Southwest, this is a member of the goosefoot family found growing
wild in nearly every part of the country in waste places. In the spring it
makes the most wonderful leafy green imaginable, cooked simply like
spinach. The older plants make a good leaf herb, particularly with beans
(it is said to counteract their afflatus). Learn to recognize and use it.

Masa Harina   The fine corn flour from which tortillas and tamales are
made. It can be seen sometimes also as fresh masa, a ready-to-use paste,
but you will more commonly find it in bags in the flour section of your
store.

Onions   Any variety of onion may be used, as you please, when it is to
be cooked. But many of these recipes call for raw onion, and the
common yellow or white onions are rather harsh for this. If you don't
have green onions or red onions at hand, the harsh flavor can be tamed a
bit by soaking chopped onion in salted ice water for 30 minutes or so.

Piñon nuts   Also called pine nuts or pignolias, these are sweet and
delicious additions to many a dish. Don't bother, however, with the
small packages usually found in markets, which are both expensive and
generally stale. Look around in health-food stores which usually sell
them in bulk, or for a fresh fall crop, and keep a supply in the
refrigerator.

Pumpkin seeds   These are also called *pepitas.* Hulled, the delicious
pale green seeds are useful for several sauces, and for general garnish and
contrast in texture. They are widely available already hulled, both salted
and unsalted. The unsalted are the ones for cooking.

Squash blossoms   These are used more often in Mexico, but were used also by early residents of the Southwest. If you have a patch of summer squash or zucchini in your garden, they are well worth bringing back into the kitchen. The blossoms to use are the males, which drop off the vine anyway. In order to determine which are male, you must pick before 10:00 A.M. as sun closes the flowers later.

Tomatillo   These are no relation to the tomato, but a member of the nightshade family, which, when husked of their papery covering, do resemble small green tomatoes. They are beautifully tart and tasty, and you are lucky if you can find them available fresh. The canned can be used interchangeably in most recipes, but they are very acid and should be drained (and a little sugar added to the recipe). Either canned or fresh are to be found in most Hispanic markets.

Tomatoes   Alas, we know all too well what has happened to the wonderful tomato. I no longer buy them fresh except when I can find ripe ones in summer farmer's markets, and I don't recommend them in any cooked recipe. Canned tomatoes—particularly the Italian plum tomatoes—are preferable any time to the tasteless pink plastic found in today's markets. For this reason I have not indicated in recipes that fresh tomatoes, if used, must of course be peeled before being chopped.

Tortillas   Luckily these are more and more available—at least the frozen, if not the fresh. Long gone are the days when you were lucky to find even canned ones, and when cookbooks called for dubious concoctions made from cornmeal. I don't know anybody, even in the Southwest, who makes them other than for very special occasions where the thicker patted tortilla is to be eaten as a bread, or used in some particular dish. They do vary widely in quality, however, so shop around all the brands until you find and settle on the very best.

Menus

Fiery Company Dinner

Avocado Slices in Rum (p. 217)
on lettuce leaves
Carne Adovada with Jicama (p. 155)
Refried Beans (p. 60)
with sour cream, Tortilla Chips (p. 7) and Jalapeño Salsa (p. 56)
Lettuce and Radish Garnish (p. 61)
Tequila Sherbet (p. 263)
Polvorones (p. 268)
Beer / Coffee

Mild Company Dinner

Avocado Cream (p. 33)
Tortilla Chips
Chicken Breasts in Pumpkinseed Sauce (p. 126)
Black Beans
with sour cream and Jalapeño Salsa (p. 56)
Lettuce and Radish Garnish (p. 61)
Bananas in Rum (p. 255)
White Wine / Coffee

Do-Ahead Company Dinner

Sally's Black Bean Soup with Tortillas (p. 41)
Trout Frosted with Guacamole (p. 122)
Rice with Toasted Piñon Nuts (p. 206)
Green Chile Salad (p. 229)
Mangoes in Orange Sauce (p. 254)
Biscochitos (p. 267)
White Wine / Coffee

Having Julia Child to Dinner

Corn in Red Chile Sauce (p. 198)
Buttered Corn Tortillas
Baked Pork Loin with Oranges (p. 143)
Garbanzo Purée (p. 204)
garnished with pumpkin seeds
Tomatillo Salad (p. 233)
on lettuce leaves
Mexican Cream with Strawberries (p. 239)
Cinnamon Crisps (p. 264)
White Wine / Coffee

Holiday Dinner

Escabeche of Shrimp (p. 25)
Oysters Phoenix (p. 26)
Avocado Consommé (p. 31)
Tortilla Chips
Turkey with Garbanzo Stuffing (p. 138)
Cranberry Relish
San Antonio Cream Peas (p. 194)
Tossed Green Salad with Piñon and Green Chile Dressing (p. 228)
Pumpkin Flan (p. 242)
White Wine / Coffee

Buffet Cocktail Party

Chile Con Queso (p. 13)
Albondigas (p. 18)
Guacamole (p. 219)
Cold Garbanzo Dip (p. 11)
Jicama Sticks (p. 15)
Green Chile Cheese Squares (p. 17)
Texas Escabeche of Vegetables (p. 63)
Oaxaca Bar Peanuts (p. 20)
Tortilla Chips
Cocktails

Buffet Dinner Party

Mission Sesame Chicken Casserole (p. 132)
Avocado and Papaya Salad (p. 218)
Refried Beans (p. 60)
Lettuce and Radish Garnish (p. 61)
Almendrado (p. 248)
Cinnamon Crisps (p. 264)
White Wine / Coffee

Vegetarians for Dinner I

Tomato Green Chile Soup (p. 36)
Cheese and Onion Enchiladas (p. 67)
with Red Chile Sauce (p. 51)
Green Stacked Enchiladas (p. 68)
Refried Beans (p. 60)
Lettuce and Radish Garnish (p. 61)
Natillas (p. 246)
Beer / Coffee

Vegetarians for Dinner II

Potato Soup with Green Chiles (p. 35)
Tortilla Chips
Bean Chimichangas (p. 85)
Aztec Pie (p. 81)
Lettuce and Radish Garnish (p. 61)
Texas Escabeche of Vegetables (p. 63)
Bananas Glazed with Guava (p. 256)
Beer / Coffee

Company Brunch

Green Chile Soufflé in a Tortilla Crust (p. 111)
Refried Beans (p. 60)
with sour cream and Jalapeño Salsa (p. 56)
Rooster's Bill (p. 236)
Coffee

Family Sunday Breakfast I

Tortas de Huevos (p. 102)
Refried Beans (p. 60)
Lettuce and Radish Garnish (p. 61)
Coffee

Family Sunday Breakfast II

Green Chilaquiles Omelet (p. 103)
Rooster's Bill (p. 236)
Coffee

Family Lunch or Supper I

Posole (p. 44)
with garnishes
Natillas (p. 246)
Beer / Coffee

Family Lunch or Supper II

Everyday Tostadas (p. 86)
Quick Chocolate Rum Mousse (p. 245)
Beer / Coffee

Family Dinner I

Potato Soup with Green Chiles (p. 35)
Tucson Cassoulet (p. 150)
Lettuce and Radish Garnish (p. 61)
Flan (p. 240)
Beer / Coffee

Family Dinner II

Tomato Green Chile Soup (p. 36)
Cumin Liver (p. 159)
Calabacitas (p. 189)
Cantaloupe Ice (p. 259)
Cinnamon Crisps (p. 264)
White Wine / Coffee

Index

Albondigas, 18

Albuquerque Baked Chicken
Breasts, 125

Almendrado, 248

Appetizers, 5–27
  Bean Dip I, 9
  Bean Dip II, 10
  Chile Cashews, 19
  Chile Con Queso, 13
  Cold Gazpacho Dip, 11
  Green Chile Cheese Squares, 17
  Green Chile Won Tons, 16
  Gus's Mousse, 12
  Jicama Sticks, 15
  Nachos, 8
  Oaxaca Bar Peanuts, 20
  Oysters Phoenix, 26
  Pickled Jalapeños Stuffed with
    Walnut Cheese, 23
  Ripe Olives Stuffed with Green
    Chile, 24
  Texas Caviar, 14
  Texas Gazpacho, 34

Avocado
  Aztec Soup, 38
  Chilled Avocado Soup, 32
  Green Bean and Avocado Salad,
    220
  Guacamole, 219
  Gus's Mousse, 12

Hot Avocado Salad, 221

Avocado and Papaya Salad, 218

Avocado and Tomato Aspic, 224

Avocado Consommé, 31

Avocado Cream, 33

Avocado Enchiladas, 72

Avocado Mousse, 222

Avocado Sherbet, 260

Avocado Slices in Rum, 217

Avocado Soufflé, 251

Aztec Pie, 81

Aztec Soup, 38

Baked Pork Loin with Oranges,
  143

Bananas Glazed with Guava, 256

Bananas in Rum, 255

Barbecue Chicken, 186

Barbecue Shrimp, 185

Barbecue Spareribs, 182

Barbecues, 177–86

Bean Chimichangas, 85

Bean Dip I, 9

Bean Dip II, 10

Beans
  Chiles Rellenos with Beans, 203
  Cooked Pinto Beans, 59
  Eggs Baked with Beans, 108
  Garbanzo and Chorizo Casserole,
    148

Beans, cont'd.
  Garbanzo Purée, 204
  Green Garbanzo Salad, 235
  Pinto Bean Soup, 40
  Purée of Garbanzo Soup, 42
  Ranchero Bean Soup, 39
  Refried Beans, 60
  Rolled Bean Enchiladas, 73
  Sally's Black Bean Soup with
    Tortillas, 41
  Stacked Bean Enchiladas, 74
  Texas Caviar, 14
  Tucson Cassoulet, 150
Beef
  Albondigas, 18
  Bill Benton's Chili Burgers, 179
  Carne Adovada, 154
  Carne Asada, 177
  Chile Meat Sauce, 54
  Cumin Liver, 159
  John Bigelow's Hamburgers
    with Guacamole, 180
  Meatball Soup, 43
  New Mexican Meatloaf, 158
  Pedernales River Chili, 46
  Picadillo, 153
  Santa Fe Steak, 156
  Stew with Squash, 160
  Stuffed Chile Meatloaf, 157
  Taco Salad, 230

Beef Filling, 173
Bill Benton's Chile Burgers, 179
Biscochitos, 267
Black beans
  Sally's Black Bean Soup with
    Tortillas, 41
  Tucson Cassoulet, 150
Black-eyed peas
  Texas Caviar, 14
Bread
  Corn Tortillas, 213
  Flour Tortillas, 213
  Navajo Fry Bread, 212
  Texas Spoonbread, 209
  Tortillas, 210
Burritos, 83

Calabacitas, 189
Calabacitas Soup, 37
Cantaloupe Ice, 259
Carne Adovada, 154
Carne Adovada Tostadas, 90
Carne Adovada with Jicama, 155
Carne Asada, 177
Carnitas, 144
Casseroles
  Chicken with Pumpkinseed
    Sauce, 130
  Chiles Rellenos, 202

Garbanzo and Chorizo Casserole, 148

Mission Sesame Chicken, 132

Spanish Chicken, 131

Tamale Pies, 167–74

Cauliflower Frosted with Guacamole, 223

Cheese

Chile Con Queso, 13

Green Chile Cheese Squares, 17

Cheese and Onion Enchiladas, 67

Cheese Tostadas with Flour Tortillas, 93

Chicken, 125–37

Albuquerque Baked Chicken Breasts, 125

Barbecue, 186

Calabacitas Soup, 37

Emmanuel's Chicken Crepes with Green Chile Sauce, 134

Fried Chicken with Fresh Salsa, 128

Mission Sesame Chicken Casserole, 132

Spanish Chicken Casserole, 131

Chicken and Green Chile Pie, 82

Chicken Breasts in Pumpkinseed Sauce, 126

Chicken Casserole with Pumpkinseed Sauce, 130

Chicken Cheese Tamale Pie, 170

Chicken Filling, 172

Chicken Mole, 137

Chicken Mole Enchiladas, 80

Chicken Tacos with Green Chile Sauce, 96

Chicken with Green Chile Sauce, 129

Chicken with Green Chiles and Sour Cream, 136

Chile Cashews, 19

Chile Con Queso, 13

Chile Meat Sauce, 54

Chiles Rellenos, 200

Chiles Rellenos Casserole, 202

Chiles Rellenos with Beans, 203

Chili, Pedernales River, 46

Chilled Avocado Soup, 32

Chimichangas, 84

Chocolate

Mexican Chocolate Ice Cream, 261

Mole Sauce, 57

Quick Chocolate Rum Mousse, 245

Quick Mole Sauce, 58

Chorizo, 146

Chorizo Chilaquiles, 152

Chorizo Tostadas, 89

Cinnamon Crisps, 264

Coconut Flan, 244
Cold Garbanzo Dip, 11
Cooked Pinto Beans, 59
Cookies
  Biscochitos, 267
  Polvorones, 268
Corn
  Aztec Soup, 38
  Green Corn Cakes in Red Chile
    Sauce, 199
Corn Fritters, 197
Corn in Red Chile Sauce, 198
Corn Tortillas, 213
Corn with Green Chiles, 196
Cream Cheese Enchiladas, 71
Cumin Liver, 159
Cynthia's Tostadas with Sour
  Cream, 88

Desert Rabbit, 164
Desserts, 239–68
  Almendrado, 248
  Avocado Sherbet, 260
  Avocado Soufflé, 251
  Bananas Glazed with Guava,
    256
  Bananas in Rum, 255
  Biscochitos, 267
  Cantaloupe Ice, 258
  Cinnamon Crisps, 264

Coconut Flan, 244
Flan, 240
Guava Empanadas, 265
Mango Floating Island, 250
Mango Ice with Rum Tango
  Topping, 262
Mangoes in Orange Sauce, 254
Mexican Chocolate Ice Cream,
  261
Mexican Cream with
  Strawberries, 239
Natillas, 246
Orange Slices with Avocado
  Cream, 258
Pineapple in White Wine, 257
Polvorones, 268
Pumpkin Flan, 242
Quick Chocolate Rum Mousse,
  245
Quince Cheese, 253
Sopaipillas, 266
Tequila Sherbet, 263
Dips
  Bean Dip I, 9
  Bean Dip II, 10
  Chile Con Queso, 13
  Cold Garbanzo, 11
  Guacamole, 219
  Gus's Mousse, 12
  Texas Caviar, 14

Eggs, 101–11
  Avocado Soufflé, 251
  Green Chilaquiles Omelet, 104
  Green Chile Soufflé in a Tortilla
    Crust, 111
  Huevos Rancheros, 101
  Scrambled Eggs with Chorizo,
    110
  Scrambled Eggs with Tortillas,
    109
  Shirred Eggs in Green Chile
    Cups, 106
  Tortas de Huevos, 102
Eggs Baked with Beans, 108
Eggs in Spanish Sauce, 107
Eggs with Stuffed Green Chiles,
  103
El Paso Stacked Enchiladas, 75
Emmanuel's Chicken Crepes with
  Green Chile Sauce, 134
Enchiladas
  Avocado, 72
  Cheese and Onion, 67
  Chicken Mole, 80
  Cream Cheese, 71
  El Paso Stacked, 75
  Pork, 78
  Rolled Bean, 73
  Sour Cream, 70
  Stacked Bean, 74

  Stacked Green, 68
  Texas Turkey Enchilada
    Casserole, 76
Escabeche of Shrimp, 25
Everyday Tacos, 95
Everyday Tostadas, 86

Fish, 115–22
  Barbecue Shrimp, 185
  Escabeche of Shrimp, 25
  Orange Snapper, 120
  Red Snapper with Chile Orange
    Sauce, 117
  Seviche, 121
  Swordfish Steaks with Green
    Chile Sauce, 116
  Trout Frosted with Guacamole,
    122
Fish Casserole with Chile and
  Wine, 118
Fish Fillets with Parsley and Piñon
  Sauce, 115
Flan, 240
  Coconut, 244
  Pumpkin, 242
Flour Tortillas, 213
Flour Tostadas with Chile Meat
  Sauce, 94
Fresh Salsa, 55

Fried Chicken with Fresh Salsa, 128

Garbanzo and Chorizo Casserole, 148
Garbanzo Purée, 204
Garbanzos
   Green Garbanzo Salad, 235
   Purée of Garbanzo Soup, 42
Garnishes, 61–63
   Lettuce and Radish Garnish, 61
   Parsleyed Onion Rings, 62
   Texas Escabeche of Vegetables, 63
Gazpacho, Texas, 34
Grilled Lamb Patties, 181
Grilled Steaks, 178
Green Bean and Avocado Salad, 220
Green Beans, New Mexican, 193
Green Chilaquiles Omelet, 104
Green Chile Cheese Squares, 17
Green Chile Salad, 229
Green Chile Sauce, 53
Green Chile Soufflé in a Tortilla Crust, 111
Green Chile Won Tons, 16
Green Chiles
   Aztec Pie, 81

Chicken and Green Chile Pie, 82
Chicken Tacos with Green Chile Sauce, 96
Chicken with Green Chiles and Sour Cream, 136
Chile con Queso, 13
Chile Meat Sauce, 54
Chiles Rellenos, 200
Chiles Rellenos Casserole, 202
Chiles Rellenos with Beans, 203
Eggs with Stuffed Green Chiles, 103
El Paso Stacked Enchiladas, 75
Emmanuel's Chicken Crepes with Green Chile Sauce, 134
Green Chilaquiles Omelet, 104
Green Rice, 207
Huevos Rancheros, 101
Ripe Olives Stuffed with Green Chile, 24
Saffron Rice Stuffed with Green Chiles, 205
Shirred Eggs in Green Chile Cups, 106
Stacked Green Enchiladas, 68
Stuffed Green Chile Salad, 232
Swordfish Steaks with Green Chile Sauce, 116

Texas Escabeche of Vegetables, 63
Tomato Green Chile Soup, 36
Green Corn Cakes in Red Chile Sauce, 199
Green Garbanzo Salad, 235
Green Rice, 207
Guacamole, 219
Guacamole Rice Ring, 208
Guava Empanadas, 265
Guava Paste with Cream Cheese, 252
Gus's Mousse, 12

Hot Avocado Salad, 221
Huevos Rancheros, 101

Indian Nut Mix, 22

Jalapeño Salsa, 56
Jicama
    Rooster's Bill, 236
Jicama Sautéed with Coriander, 192
Jicama Sticks, 15
John Bigelow's Hamburgers with Guacamole, 180

Lamb
    Grilled Lamb Patties, 181

Leg of Lamb in Chile and Wine Sauce, 162
    Stew with Squash, 160
Lamb Chops, 184
Lamb Ribs with Red Chile Sauce, 161
Leg of Lamb in Chile and Wine Sauce, 162
Lettuce and Radish Garnish, 61

Mango Floating Island, 250
Mango Ice with Rum Tango Topping, 262
Mangoes in Orange Sauce, 254
Meatball Soup, 43
Meatballs
    Albondigas, 18
Mexican Chocolate Ice Cream, 261
Mexican Cream with Strawberries, 239
Mission Sesame Chicken Casserole, 132
Mole Sauce, 57
Mole Sauce, Quick, 58
Mousse, Quick Chocolate Rum, 245

Nachos, 8
Natillas, 246
Navajo Fry Bread, 212

New Mexican Green Beans, 193
New Mexican Meatloaf, 158
Nopalitos, 191
Nuts
    Chile Cashews, 19
    Indian Nut Mix, 22
    Oaxaca Bar Peanuts, 20

Oaxaca Bar Peanuts, 20
Orange Slices with Avocado
    Cream, 258
Orange Snapper, 120
Oysters Phoenix, 26

Parsleyed Onion Rings, 62
Peanuts
    Oaxaca Bar Peanuts, 20
Peas, San Antonio Cream, 194
Pedernales River Chili, 46
Picadillo, 153
Pickled Jalapeños Stuffed with
    Walnut Cheese, 23
Pineapple in White Wine, 257
Pinto Bean Soup, 40
Pinto Beans
    Chiles Rellenos with Beans, 203
    Cooked Pinto Beans, 59
    Eggs Baked with Beans, 108
    Ranchero Bean Soup, 39
    Refried Beans, 60

Rolled Bean Enchiladas, 73
Stacked Bean Enchiladas, 74
Tucson Cassoulet, 150
Polvorones, 268
Pork
    Albondigas, 18
    Baked Pork Loin with Oranges,
        143
    Barbecue Spareribs, 182
    Carne Adovada, 154
    Carnitas, 144
    Chorizo, 146
    Chorizo Chilaquiles, 152
    Garbanzo and Chorizo Casserole,
        148
    Meatball Soup, 43
    Picadillo, 153
    Posole, 44
    Spicy Pork Chops, 183
    Tinza, 145
    Tucson Cassoulet, 150
Pork Chops with Kidney Beans,
    147
Pork Enchiladas, 78
Pork Filling, 174
Posole, 44
Potato Soup with Green Chiles, 35
Pumpkin Flan, 242
Purée of Garbanzo Soup, 42

Quelites, 195
Quesadillas, 97
Quick Chocolate Rum Mousse, 245
Quick Mole Sauce, 58
Quick Red Chile Sauce, 52
Quince Cheese, 253

Rabbit, Desert, 164
Ranchero Bean Soup, 39
Red Chile Sauce, 51
Red Chiles
  Carne Adovada, 154
  Corn in Red Chile Sauce, 198
  Green Corn Cakes in Red Chile Sauce, 199
  Huevos Rancheros, 101
  Lamb Ribs with Red Chile Sauce, 161
  Mission Sesame Chicken Casserole, 132
  Texas Turkey Enchilada Casserole, 76
  Tortas de Huevos, 102
Red Snapper with Chile Orange Sauce, 117
Refried Beans, 60
Rice
  Green, 207
  Guacamole Rice Ring, 208

Saffron Rice with Stuffed Green Chiles, 205
Rice with Toasted Piñon Nuts, 206
Ripe Olives Stuffed with Green Chile, 24
Rolled Bean Enchiladas, 73
Rooster's Bill, 236

Saffron Rice with Stuffed Green Chiles, 205
Salads, 217–36
  Avocado and Papaya Salad, 218
  Avocado and Tomato Aspic, 224
  Avocado Mousse, 222
  Avocado Slices in Rum, 217
  Cauliflower Frosted with Guacamole, 223
  Green Bean and Avocado Salad, 220
  Green Chile Salad, 229
  Green Garbanzo Salad, 235
  Guacamole, 219
  Hot Avocado Salad, 221
  Rooster's Bill, 236
  Stuffed Green Chile Salad, 232
  Taco, 230
  Tomatillo Salad, 233
  Tomatoes Stuffed with Celery and Piñon Nuts, 234

Tossed Green Salad with Piñon
  and Green Chile Dressing,
  228
Tossed Salad with Avocado
  Dressing, 227
Tossed Salad with Chile
  Croutons, 226
Sally's Black Bean Soup with
  Tortillas, 41
Salsa
  Fresh, 55
  Jalapeño, 56
San Antonio Cream Peas, 194
Santa Fe Steak, 156
Sauces, 49–60
  Chile Meat Sauce, 54
  Fresh Salsa, 55
  Green Chile Sauce, 53
  Jalapeño Salsa, 56
  Mole, 57
  Quick Mole, 58
  Quick Red Chile, 52
  Red Chile, 51
Scrambled Eggs with Chorizo, 110
Scrambled Eggs with Tortillas,
  109
Seafood, 115–22
  Escabeche of Shrimp, 25
  Oysters Phoenix, 26
Seviche, 121

Shirred Eggs in Green Chile Cups,
  106
Shrimp
  Barbecue, 185
  Escabeche of, 25
Sopaipillas, 266
Soup, 29–47
  Avocado Consommé, 31
  Avocado Cream, 33
  Aztec, 38
  Calabacitas, 37
  Chilled Avocado Soup, 32
  Meatball, 43
  Pedernales River Chili, 46
  Pinto Bean, 40
  Posole, 44
  Potato Soup with Green Chiles,
    35
  Purée of Garbanzo Soup, 42
  Ranchero Bean, 39
  Sally's Black Bean Soup with
    Tortillas, 41
  Texas Gazpacho, 34
  Tomato Green Chile Soup, 36
Sour Cream Enchiladas, 70
Spicy Pork Chops, 183
Squash
  Aztec Soup, 38
  Calabacitas, 189
  Calabacitas Soup, 37

Stew with, 160
Squash Flower Pancakes, 190
Squash Flower Tostadas, 92
Stacked Bean Enchiladas, 74
Stacked Green Enchiladas, 68
Stew with Squash, 160
Strawberries
    Mexican Cream with
        Strawberries, 239
Stuffed Chile Meatloaf, 157
Stuffed Green Chile Salad, 232
Swordfish Steaks with Green Chile
    Sauce, 116

Taco Salad, 230
Tacos
    Chicken Tacos with Green Chile
        Sauce, 96
    Everyday, 95
Tamale Pies, 167–74
    Beef Filling, 173
    Chicken Cheese Tamale Pie, 170
    Chicken Filling, 172
    Pork Fillings, 174
    Tamale Mixture I, 167
    Tamale Mixture II, 168
    Tamale Mixture III, 169
Tequila Sherbet, 263
Texas Caviar, 14
Texas Escabeche of Vegetables, 63

Texas Gazpacho, 34
Texas Spoonbread, 209
Texas Turkey Enchilada Casserole,
    76
Tinga, 145
Tomatillo Salad, 233
Tomato Green Chile Soup, 36
Tomatoes
    Avocado and Tomato Aspic, 224
    Fresh Salsa, 55
    Mole Sauce, 57
    Pedernales River Chili, 46
    Texas Gazpacho, 34
Tomatoes Stuffed with Celery and
    Piñon Nuts, 234
Tortas de Huevos, 102
Tortilla Bread, 210
Tortilla Chips, 7
Tossed Green Salad with Piñon and
    Green Chile Dressing, 228
Tossed Salad with Avocado
    Dressing, 227
Tossed Salad with Chile Croutons,
    226
Tostadas
    Carne Adovada, 90
    Cheese Tostadas with Flour
        Tortillas, 93
    Chorizo, 89

Cynthia's Tostadas with Sour
Cream, 88
Everyday, 86
Flour Tostadas with Chile Meat
Sauce, 94
Squash Flower, 92
Tostadas with Beans and Chorizo,
91
Trout Frosted with Guacamole,
122
Tucson Cassoulet, 150
Turkey
Calabacitas Soup, 37
Texas Turkey Enchilada
Casserole, 76
Turkey and Green Chile Pie, 82
Turkey Casserole with
Pumpkinseed Sauce, 130
Turkey Filling for Tamale Pie, 172
Turkey Mole, 137
Turkey Mole Enchiladas, 80
Turkey with Garbanzo Stuffing,
138

Turkey with Green Chiles and Sour
Cream, 136

Veal Chops, 182
Vegetables, 189–99
Calabacitas, 189
Corn Fritters, 197
Corn in Red Chile Sauce, 198
Corn with Green Chiles, 196
Green Corn Cakes in Red Chile
Sauce, 199
Jicama Sautéed with Coriander,
192
Lettuce and Radish Garnish, 61
New Mexican Green Beans, 193
Nopalitos, 191
Parsleyed Onion Rings, 62
San Antonio Cream Peas, 194
Squash with Flower Pancakes,
190
Texas Escabeche of Vegetables,
63